THE GOOD GUYS

THE GOOD GUYS

50 HEROES WHO CHANGED the WORLD with KINDNESS

ROB KEMP   PAUL BLOW

wren
&rook

Wren & Rook
An imprint of
Hachette Children's Group
Part of Hodder & Stoughton
Carmelite House
50 Victoria Embankment
London EC4Y 0DZ

An Hachette UK Company
www.hachette.co.uk
www.hachettechildrens.co.uk

Publishing Director: Debbie Foy
Senior Editor: Liza Miller
Art Director: Laura Hambleton
Designer: We Mean This

Printed in Germany

'Be kind
whenever
possible.

It is always
possible.'

TENZIN GYATSO, 14TH DALAI LAMA

CONTENTS

INTRODUCTION

If you were to write a list of the people you most admire, how would you begin? With your friends and family, the people who set a great example for you every day? Maybe you'd include teachers, coaches, group leaders or even celebrities. One thing is certain – your list would be fascinating, unique to you and perhaps even surprising to anyone else reading it.

This book is just such a list – of the good guys from throughout history who inspire me every day. It includes sports stars, politicians, inventors and business leaders, each one extraordinary, and each of whom has helped to make the world a better place.

It's a strange thing – kindness and generosity aren't always the traits that spring to mind when people talk about 'great men'. In fact, men are much more likely to be celebrated for being tough, powerful, successful or wealthy (or all four!) than they are for being nice. But I wanted to show that it's actually possible to be all five of these things. So, while some of the good guys in this book have been powerful, tough or successful, here we celebrate their

concern for others, and their desire to make society fairer and better for everyone.

Choosing which 50 men would make the cut wasn't as straightforward as I first thought. What *is* kindness, after all? But when I considered it, I decided that kindness could mean anything from consoling a sporting opponent after a tough match to speaking out against injustice, or even founding a company with the potential to save all of humankind. There are so many ways to do good in the world. It also made me think, though, about how difficult it is to be nice 100 per cent of the time. Some of my 'good guys' haven't always been good and kind. I wanted to celebrate them for their acts of kindness, without ignoring other aspects of their lives. I hope I've been successful.

The men in this book are all here for vastly different reasons. Some had day jobs with nothing at all to do with kindness, such as competing in the ruthless world of professional sports. Athletes Muhammad Ali and Colin Kaepernick have both used their fame and success as a platform to effect change in society, and to raise awareness of racism and injustice. And others have faced huge challenges in their own lives and decided to help those in similar situations. Christopher Reeve and Louis Braille both had disabilities, and were inspired by this to make a difference within their communities.

Some of these heroes have had to be extremely brave to do good, such as Oskar Schindler and Raoul Wallenberg, who both risked their lives to save complete strangers from almost certain death. But some have only had to endure inconvenience to help others – Aussie James Harrison has donated samples of his rare blood every few weeks for almost his entire life. He even finds donation centres when he goes on holiday! Being kind can often mean showing your softer side too, which isn't always easy. Professor Green and

Patrick Stewart are tearing down harmful stereotypes that men should be strong and silent, and giving guys both young and old the confidence to be honest about their feelings when times are tough.

If you've ever dreamed about being rich and successful, then you might have thought about enormous mansions and flashy cars, but maybe not about using your wealth to help other people, like some of these good guys. Lionel Messi, the multi-millionaire footballer, does all he can to help sick and dying children around the world. Pierre Toussaint became wealthy after escaping slavery, and devoted his life to assisting those in desperate need. And pop star George Michael was determined to help people in any way he could, but gave his time and money to deserving causes in total secrecy, so he was never a distraction.

What all these good guys have in common, though, is that they show us the extraordinary power of kindness. So if you believe in fighting for a worthy cause, standing up for what you believe is right, in fairness and the power of good, then I hope you will find the men within these pages as compelling, unique, surprising and inspiring as I do.

Rob Kemp

CONFUCIUS

Philosopher of Kindness

If anyone can be said to have written the book on kindness, it's Confucius. He was a teacher who lived around 2,500 years ago in China, but even today he is admired for his ideas and writings about the importance of family, respect and kindness. Ever heard the phrase, 'Do not do to others what you do not want done to you'? That was Confucius's golden rule, and it means that we should treat other people with the kindness that we'd like them to show us.

We know very little about Confucius's life, but his family were probably members of the aristocracy who had become impoverished by the time he was born. He was a dedicated teacher but led an otherwise unremarkable life, in contrast to the legacy he left behind. But in many ways, his quiet life reveals much of what he taught. Confucius firmly believed that any one person is capable of changing the world, and that we can all make ourselves better if we work hard at it every day.

When Confucius was writing, his homeland, China, was in turmoil. Battles raged between different warlords and the rule of law was breaking down, so Confucius decided to dedicate his whole life to learning and teaching about how to improve society. When the wars in China came to an end and the new rulers looked for the best way to run the country, they used Confucius's ideas.

Confucius believed that the country's leaders should be humble and show compassion towards those who followed them. Rather than seeking out greater power or money, they should take decisions for the nation based on what is right and good. He also taught that the young should look after their elders. He encouraged people to behave kindly and respectfully in everything they did, even down to how they ate a meal.

Whilst his ideas certainly haven't always been perfectly applied, the way of life that many people follow today in China and beyond – particularly in other Asian countries such as Korea, Japan and Vietnam – stems from Confucius's ancient wisdom written down more than two millennia ago.

551-479 BCE

'The more man
meditates upon
good thoughts,
the better will
be his world
and the world
at large.'

LEONARDO
DA VINCI
Brave Polymath

∙∙

Mention the name Leonardo da Vinci and many people usually picture the Italian artist's most famous painting, the *Mona Lisa*. Others think of his scientific genius, such as his ideas for flying machines that were centuries ahead of their time. However, few people know that kindness was threaded throughout Leonardo's life. Although details of his personal history are rather patchy, we have evidence from his notebooks and journals that help biographers piece together his complex character.

Leonardo depicted the true horrors of warfare in his painting *The Battle of Anghiari*. So it may surprise you to learn that he accepted commissions from rich Italian nobles to design weapons for their warring armies. However, some experts believe that in a mischievous masterstroke, Leonardo took those jobs so that he could provide designs with intentional errors in them, creating weapons that could never harm a human being.

Leonardo didn't want animals to get hurt either, so he refused to eat meat. That may not seem like much of a big deal today, but in sixteenth-century Florence, Italy, where meat was considered essential to a person's diet and religious duty, being vegetarian was radical. But he didn't stop there – Leonardo was so passionate about animal welfare that he bought caged birds destined to become food or pets, just so he could set them free.

As well as being an extraordinary polymath, Leonardo was a brave man who had gay relationships at a time when homosexual acts were illegal. One of his studio assistants, Salai, served him for 30 years and was also his lover. Leonardo remembered him in his will by gifting him the *Mona Lisa*, a valuable painting even then, as well as half his precious vineyard.

We have learned much about Leonardo from his notebooks. In them, he despaired of men who valued their worth by their riches and brutality. Leonardo believed that humility and compassion were much greater measures of a man. He is celebrated today for genius that was far ahead of its time – but his capacity for kindness is just as inspirational.

∙∙

1452-1519

DE LAS CASAS

Human Rights Advocate

As a young man, Bartolomé played a part in the cruel and murderous conquest of the Americas by Spanish settlers. But as he grew older, he had an epiphany and changed his ways to become a pioneer of human rights and a protector of those he once persecuted.

Bartolomé's father had sailed with the explorer Christopher Columbus, and was one of the first conquerors of the Caribbean. The Spanish settlers treated the indigenous people who lived there as if they were less than human, enslaving them and robbing them of their land.

At first, Bartolomé supported the way the Spanish ruled over the Americas. The money his father made from keeping slaves paid for him to train as a priest. But Bartolomé soon struggled to be a man of the church while also supporting such atrocities.

In 1514, after witnessing yet another slaughter of innocent people on the island of Cuba, he said enough was enough. Bartolomé freed the slaves on his own land and called for his peers to do the same. When the other colonists refused, Bartolomé boarded a ship sailing for Spain to plead with the king to put an end to the brutality. The king died before they could speak, but that didn't stop Bartolomé from calling for the people of the Americas to be freed from slavery. He made a big mistake when he suggested that African people could be used as slaves instead, but he soon realised how wrong that would be. From then on, he argued that everyone, whatever their background, was a human being and deserved equal respect.

When Spain's rulers changed the laws to meet Bartolomé's demands, he began to receive death threats from the colonists. They became even angrier when the young priest refused to perform religious services for them unless they freed all their slaves.

Bartolomé spent the rest of his life travelling around the Caribbean islands, South America and Spain calling for an end to slavery and brutality towards the indigenous peoples. Despite many risks to his own life, Bartolomé constantly defied those who refused to treat all humankind as equals, and became one of the world's first champions for human rights.

C. 1484-1566

RICHARD
MARTIN
Animal Rights Pioneer

Today we have laws in place that are designed to protect animals from being treated poorly, but that wasn't always the case. In Europe in the 1700s, herding sheep, cows and pigs by beating them was a common practice by owners. Other animals, including cockerels and bears, were even made to fight to the death for a crowd's entertainment.

Although many people would pay to watch cockfighting and 'bear-baiting', as it was known, others started calling for an end to the mistreatment of animals. One of those was the Irish politician Richard Martin, who was known for his kindness and especially his love of animals.

When he was asked why he was so passionate about protecting animals, Richard replied, 'Sir, an ox cannot hold a pistol!' By this he meant that because animals couldn't defend themselves against humans, he would be willing to fight to protect them from cruelty instead. And one day, he did exactly that. When Richard heard that a man had killed a dog, he became outraged and challenged him to a gunfight. The two men wounded each other with their pistols, but both survived.

Richard was a Member of the Irish Parliament, which meant he could change the law to protect animals if he could persuade enough politicians to vote for it. He campaigned in Parliament and he took to the streets, telling people to stop hurting animals for entertainment. Many people laughed at him and even drew pictures of him with donkey's ears, but he remained resolute. At that time, Ireland was part of the UK, and in 1822, King George IV passed a groundbreaking law – nicknamed Martin's Act – which meant that people who harmed farm animals would be fined or imprisoned.

Richard also helped to set up the Royal Society for the Prevention of Cruelty to Animals (RSPCA), the oldest and largest animal welfare organisation in the world. Richard died in 1834, but a year later, the practice of making animals fight for entertainment was banned in the UK for good, securing his legacy for ever.

1754-1834

WILBERFORCE

Tireless Abolitionist

The name William Wilberforce will for ever be associated with the abolition of Britain's slave trade. He was a British Member of Parliament (MP) who became aware of the horrors of slavery early in his career. William was appalled at how men and women from Africa were being taken from their homes and families, beaten and put into chains. They were then transported in filthy ships across dangerous seas before being sold to landowners in the British colonies of the Americas and the Caribbean, where they toiled for long hours for no pay.

William was so outraged by the slave trade, which operated with the full support of the British Parliament, that he considered quitting as an MP. But he was convinced by others that he could serve humanity better if he used his position of power to bring about change. He faced a fierce battle to do so.

The majority of politicians in Parliament deemed slaves to be less than human, and declared they were only useful as cheap, disposable labour. Many of them owned slaves themselves in the British colonies, or had wealthy friends who did. So when William first proposed a law to abolish the slave trade, over 160 MPs voted against it. But he was determined never to give up trying.

William took to the streets to make ordinary people aware of the harsh treatment of slaves. He also met with many of the MPs who voted against him, arguing, wheedling and debating with them to convince them to change their minds. He would present his abolition bill to Parliament again and again, persuading more and more MPs each time. After working tirelessly for decades, William once again petitioned Parliament to abolish slavery, at the age of 73. By that time, he was so frail he could barely walk.

It took the MPs months to debate it, but finally, on 26 July 1833, the majority of them voted to abolish slavery throughout all British colonies. The news was taken to William at home. He died just three days later, but he went to his grave knowing that he had finally brought about an end to the slave trade.

1759-1833

TOUSSAINT

Hairdresser and Philanthropist

Pierre Toussaint was born a slave. He vowed that when he was free, he would do all he could to help those who suffered.

Until the age of 21, Pierre was kept on a plantation on the island of Haiti with his sister Rosalie. As slaves in the household of the Bérard family, they were treated better than many others: Pierre was taught to read and write, and to speak English and French. But they were not free to leave. When the people of Haiti began to rebel against slavery, the Bérards left for New York City, USA, taking Pierre and Rosalie with them. New York was very different to the islands of the Caribbean, with new laws and opportunities. Pierre was able to work outside of the family home as a hairdresser, and when his owners died, he was set free. He had earned enough money to buy Rosalie's freedom too.

Pierre then devoted his life to helping the poor of New York City. He paid for the freedom of another slave, Juliette Noel, who became his wife. The couple adopted Rosalie's daughter after Rosalie died of tuberculosis, and soon after, the Toussaints opened up their home to other orphans and began fostering abandoned children. Pierre also arranged financial aid for refugees and, because of his language skills, helped many French-speaking immigrants to find jobs. When New York suffered an outbreak of the deadly disease cholera, Pierre repeatedly risked his own life to visit quarantine houses to nurse the sick.

Despite being a respected businessman, Pierre still encountered racist attitudes from people who believed that those born as slaves should always remain slaves. Even though he donated money towards the building of a new cathedral in the city, he was refused entry to it when it first opened because of the colour of his skin.

When Pierre died in 1853, he was buried in the cemetery of the cathedral. For many years he was forgotten, but in the twentieth century, his extraordinary kindness was recognised and began to be celebrated. In 1996, Pope John Paul II declared Pierre 'venerable'.

1766-1853

OWEN

Compassionate Industrialist

R obert Owen was a forward-thinking mill owner from Wales who devoted his career to improving the lives of working people.

In the late eighteenth century, mills were factories where textiles were produced. They were the powerhouses of Britain's Industrial Revolution, but they were also dangerous places where the workers were badly paid and harshly treated.

Robert wasn't a typical mill owner. Unlike many Victorian industrialists who were only motivated by money, he cared about the lives of the people he employed. He believed that by giving workers better conditions and building a strong sense of community, he could help create a fairer society for all.

He began putting his ideas into action when he and several business partners bought a mill in New Lanark, Scotland. He then announced a whole host of rule changes to improve the quality of his workers' lives. Robert immediately ended the practice of using children to clean the machines and instead set up the world's first infant school.

He also opened a nursery for the very young children of his employees.

Robert provided free medical care for his workers and set up shops selling items at cheaper prices so his employees could afford healthy meals. He also created parks and gardens so the people living around the mill could grow food and hold parties and concerts. Many of the things that workers take for granted today – such as having regular days off – were first started by Robert. He also insisted on a 10-hour working day at a time when 16-hour days were standard.

But not all of Robert's business partners were keen on his methods. They wanted to make more profit and eventually he was forced out. He moved to the USA where, in 1825, he created a new village based on the same humane approach as New Lanark. It wasn't as successful, so Robert returned to England and died penniless in 1858, having sacrificed all his wealth for his utopian dream. But his legacy lives on today and he remains a hero to those fighting for improved working conditions.

1771-1858

'To train and
educate the rising
generation will
at all times be
the first object
of society.'

BRAILLE

Teacher and Ingenious Inventor

Born in France, Louis was just three when he had an accident which left him completely blind. But he never allowed his blindness to stop him from achieving what he wanted in life. He was intelligent, but very modest. 'I do not suffer from our infirmity as much as others do,' he said when he started attending a school for blind children, even though he could not see at all.

At the National Institute for Blind Youth, the children learned a special code called 'night writing', invented by a man named Captain Barbier. They read it by feeling raised shapes made on paper. But the code had been created for soldiers to use in darkness, not for blind people. It was difficult to understand and even harder to write!

Louis set to work creating a new form of writing that blind people could read more easily. He spent all his spare time developing a new alphabet, often falling asleep at his desk. By the time he was 15, Louis had perfected his method. Unlike night writing, each letter could be read with only one finger.

Captain Barbier wasn't happy that a new, better system had been created – especially because it had been developed by a child. He criticised Louis's work and tried to have his own method declared the only official one. Despite this, Louis was always kind and gracious, remembering how much Captain Barbier had inspired his system.

When Louis finished his schooling at the National Institute, he was asked to stay on as a teacher. He remained there for the rest of his life. But even though Louis kept improving his Braille system, the school refused to teach it to its students or to translate any of their books into Braille.

Louis died of tuberculosis at the age of only 43. He didn't live to see his writing system in popular use, but just two years after his death, the National Institute finally adopted Braille. Today Braille is used around the world by everyone from musicians to authors. You may even have seen it yourself – Braille words appear in all sorts of places, such as banknotes, door signs and even shop tills!

1809–1852

'We must be treated as equals – and communication is the way we can bring this about.'

ABRAHAM
LINCOLN
President & Peacemaker

Abraham Lincoln had a very tough childhood, born to parents who could not read or write. The family had little money and his mum died when he was young. But Abraham would go on to become one of the greatest ever US presidents.

Once Abraham was old enough, he found a job doing hard physical labour for little pay. But he wanted a better life, and taught himself the law. He was a lawyer for 10 years before he turned his attention to politics. First in Illinois and then in Congress, Abraham supported efforts to bring an end to slavery in his country. In the USA, black people were kept as slaves and treated terribly. Abraham knew what it was like to be poor and desperate. He believed that black people were entitled to 'life, liberty and the pursuit of happiness', and that they deserved to be paid for their work.

In 1860 he was elected president. But before he'd even moved into the White House, a group of southern states left the USA to form their own nation, concerned that Abraham wanted to abolish slavery. A civil war erupted between northern states that supported the US Constitution and southern ones which wanted to expand slavery.

Two years after he was elected, Abraham signed a document called the Emancipation Proclamation, which guaranteed freedom to slaves who had managed to escape from the southern states during the civil war. Later, his signature also approved a thirteenth amendment to the Constitution. This decree outlawed slavery throughout the entire USA.

After four years of bloody conflict, Abraham's army won the civil war. He encouraged his supporters in the north to forgive those who had fought against them. He also prepared to pardon many of the southern soldiers who had been taken to prison, and made money available for southern states to repair their war damage. More than anything, Abraham wanted the USA to be one country at peace.

But just five days after the war was officially declared over, Abraham was shot dead by someone who supported slavery. He never lived to see the peace he wanted, but his empathy for his countrymen, whether friend or foe, earned him a place in history.

1809-1865

ROWNTREE

Compassionate Chocolatier

The motto of the Rowntree Society is 'From chocolate comes change'. It may seem like a strange choice for a charity which supports poor people, but the organisation was founded by the son of a greengrocer, Joseph Rowntree, who took over a chocolate factory and transformed the lives of many people living in poverty in Victorian Britain.

When Joseph was 14, he went on a trip to Ireland. The country had suffered from a terrible famine and Joseph witnessed its effects upon the local people, especially the poor. Many had starved to death, and those who had managed to survive had often had to leave their hometowns to find food. Joseph couldn't believe that such a tragedy had unfolded on an island just a short hop across the sea from his home. It was an experience that shaped his life for ever.

Joseph lived and worked during the Industrial Revolution, when new factories were being built all around Britain. Thousands of men, women and children were hired to work in them, but many factory owners paid their employees badly, and didn't pay them at all if they were injured or unwell.

Joseph was different. When he took over his father's chocolate-making business, he made it hugely successful. But he also believed in helping the poor to make their own lives better. He paid his workers fairly and devised a pension scheme so that his employees would have money when they retired. He also set up schools for the children of workers so that they could learn to read and write. But Joseph didn't just look out for his own employees. Having seen how people suffered through poverty in Ireland, he used the profits from sweets and chocolate sales to build a whole village, New Earswick near the city of York, so that other local people on low incomes could live in decent homes.

When Joseph became wealthy, he set up four charities to continue his ambition to transform society for the better. Even though almost 100 years have passed, they still work to strengthen democracy, fight injustice and improve housing for everyone in Britain.

1836-1925

FERDINAND
BUISSON
Teacher and Humanitarian

Ferdinand was born in Paris, France, in 1841. A bright student who left school early to support his family after the death of his father, Ferdinand always believed in the power of education. He dreamed of becoming a teacher and eventually managed to complete his studies.

After years of teaching in Switzerland, Ferdinand refused a prestigious job as a professor and became the head of a Paris orphanage instead, choosing to teach the capital city's most impoverished children. He knew what it was like to be a child without a parent and he wanted to give the orphans a better chance in life. Ferdinand's excellent reputation as a teacher and a caring man meant he was asked to manage French schools, and in 1879 he was appointed the national director of primary education. Ferdinand passionately believed that learning could change lives, so he made education free for primary-age children. He also came to the aid of people who were being persecuted, including a Jewish soldier named Alfred Dreyfus who had been wrongly accused of

treason. Campaigning on Alfred's behalf, Ferdinand helped secure his freedom and to establish the French League for Human Rights. It was Ferdinand's first taste of politics, and before long he was elected to the French Parliament. But only men were allowed to vote in elections at the time, and Ferdinand believed that was wrong. He used his voice in Parliament to campaign on behalf of women who weren't able to speak in the debates.

The First World War raged between 1914 and 1918 and ended with the Treaty of Versailles. It was a peace agreement that required Germany to make lots of promises, and many people, including Ferdinand, thought it demanded too much. They worried that another war might erupt as a result, so Ferdinand and others began arranging regular conversations between France and Germany, trying to maintain peace. Even in his 80s, he spoke at schools and public halls in both countries, hoping to prevent warfare from ever happening again. Ferdinand was awarded the Nobel Peace Prize for his efforts in 1927, five years before his death.

1841-1932

NANSEN

Polar Explorer & Diplomat

The ever-intrepid Fridtjof Nansen went from being a Norwegian champion skier and record-breaking polar explorer to saving the lives of millions of people.

Fridtjof had been part of the first team to ski across the vast Arctic wastes of Greenland, surviving temperatures of around −45°C to do so. As an intrepid explorer, he also made an attempt to reach the North Pole, breaking the record for the most northerly point reached at that time. These adventures gave Fridtjof an appetite for challenge and a resolve to keep going even when the odds were stacked against him. Such skills proved particularly useful when he became a diplomat for Norway.

One of Fridtjof's first diplomatic missions took place during the First World War, when American and British warships formed a sea blockade to stop food supplies from reaching the German army. Fridtjof discovered that Norwegian civilians were starving as a result, and he went to the USA to convince the commanders to lift the blockade. They were persuaded by Fridtjof's plea and started to allow food to travel to Norway again. This one act alone may have saved tens of thousands of innocent people from death.

But Fridtjof didn't stop there: when the war ended, he worked tirelessly to ensure that 450,000 prisoners of war held by different armies were sent home. The soldiers were stranded around the world and needed to return to 26 different countries, so making the arrangements was a formidable task.

After that success, Fridtjof was appointed the High Commissioner for Prisoners of War by the League of Nations, a new international organisation that had been created after the First World War to try and maintain peace. Fridtjof's job was to help people from war-torn countries escape to safer places. But a lot of these refugees didn't have paperwork that allowed them to cross national borders. Ingeniously, Fridtjof created a special passport that guaranteed safe passage for them. The Nansen passport saved the lives of 22 million people and led to Fridtjof being presented with the Nobel Peace Prize.

1861-1930

'The difficult
is what takes
a little time.
The impossible
is what takes
a little longer.'

MANNERHEIM

Military Leader & Nation Defender

At the outbreak of the Second World War in 1939, Gustaf Mannerheim, the commander of Finland's army, found himself and his country in a dangerous situation. The Soviet Union had invaded Finland. Gustaf's forces managed to keep the Soviets at bay for almost a year, but his army couldn't hold out indefinitely. Desperate, Gustaf reached out to Nazi Germany. The Nazis offered to help defend Finland from the Soviets, but at a price. They wanted Gustaf to hand over any Jewish people who lived in Finland so they could be deported to death camps.

Gustaf refused. Jewish men were risking their lives in the Finnish army, and he had no intention of letting the Nazis take them. So he began walking a dangerous tightrope: he agreed that Finnish troops would fight with Nazi soldiers to keep the Soviet Union out of Finland, but he refused to be their formal ally. At times Gustaf found himself shaking hands with the Nazi leader Adolf Hitler whilst handing a lifeline to the Jews Hitler wished to exterminate, secretly transporting Jewish civilians out of Finland to safety in Sweden.

The Jewish soldiers of Finland bravely continued to defend their country, despite having to fight alongside the Nazis. Gustaf did everything he could to support them: at the front line, the Finnish army even set up a synagogue for Jewish soldiers to pray in, within sight of the Nazi base camp. Saving his country required Gustaf to make some agonising decisions, including handing over Soviet prisoners of war to the Nazis, knowing that they were likely being sent to their deaths.

Some leaders might have had a hard time persuading their country that this delicate diplomacy was the way to survive, but Gustaf had the support of Finland. As well as being a skilled military leader, he had spent the years following the First World War running the Finnish Red Cross and founding the Mannerheim League for Child Welfare. At the end of the Second World War, Gustaf went on to become President of Finland. He is remembered as a national hero who managed to keep his country and all its citizens, regardless of their religion, safe when stronger enemies surrounded it on all sides.

1867-1951

EINSTEIN

Scientist & Truth Teller

Albert Einstein once said that 'Only a life lived for others is a life worthwhile'. Although he devoted his career to solving mathematical mysteries, he was also a deeply compassionate man who used his fame to draw attention to racial discrimination and change people's attitudes.

Born in Germany in 1879, Albert became world-famous for his scientific achievements. He was awarded the Nobel Prize in 1922 for his discoveries in physics, but when the Nazis came to power, they discredited him and his work because he was Jewish. They removed the books Albert had written from library shelves and burned them in the streets. Then they offered a reward to anyone who would turn him over to their execution squads.

Albert fled Germany to live in Britain and the USA, but even though he reached safety himself, that didn't stop him caring about the plight of others. In the USA, Albert spent much of his time contacting universities around the world, pleading with them to offer places to Jewish scientists who were being persecuted in Germany. He saved the lives of at least 1,000 academics by convincing the Turkish government to employ them.

Albert was haunted by the horrors he'd seen committed against Jewish people back in Germany, and he was enraged by the way black people were being treated in the United States. When a famous opera singer was refused a room at a hotel because of her skin colour, Albert invited her to stay with his family. He was nervous about speaking in public, but when universities asked him to visit and accept an award, Albert overcame his nerves to stand up in front of hundreds of people and decry racial injustice.

His scientific genius paved the way for the development of extremely powerful weapons called atomic bombs. But Albert regretted the way his discoveries had been used for warfare, and spent his remaining years calling for the abolition of these weapons. Sadly he didn't manage to achieve that – but his work on behalf of victims of discrimination meant that he lived a life that truly was worthwhile.

1879-1955

'The ideals that have lighted my way ... have been Kindness, Beauty, and Truth.'

JOHN

FLYNN

Medical Pioneer

No matter where illness or accidents occur in the vast wilderness of Australia known as 'the bush', people living there can access medical help thanks to John Flynn.

As a young man, John studied to be a preacher at a church in the city of Melbourne and went to teach Bible classes to people living on remote farms. But he soon discovered that the people of the bush needed help in all sorts of ways, especially if they became unwell. There were no hospitals or even doctors in these isolated areas. The closest medical aid was often hundreds of kilometres away and could only be reached by horse and cart, or on camels. Many patients didn't survive the long, perilous journey.

John compiled a report about the needs of the people living and working in remote places and used it to elicit funds from the church to pay for the first bush hospital. John dreamed that one day the bush would be a safe place for people to live, but he knew that the lack of communications and transport meant that many people who got sick were

dying unnecessarily. When an Australian pilot fighting in the First World War wrote to John and suggested that aeroplanes could be used to bring medical aid to people in the bush, John saw a way to realise his ambition.

He began asking businesses, churches and hospitals for funds to create the world's first air ambulance service. After 10 years of non-stop campaigning, John finally raised enough money to employ the very first 'Flying Doctor', who started work in 1928. In that first year alone, the doctor visited 255 patients afflicted by everything from typhoid fever to gunshot wounds.

Today, the Royal Flying Doctor Service has a fleet of 69 aircraft as well as 24 air bases. In addition to thousands of flights undertaken every year, almost 90,000 patients a year call the service for medical advice over the phone. Countless lives have been saved in the 90-year history of the Flying Doctors, and they all owe thanks to John Flynn and a heroic pilot from the First World War, who had a dream and made it happen.

1880-1951

'If you start
something
worthwhile,
nothing can
stop it.'

GUTTMAN

Attitude-Shifting Doctor

Ludwig was born in Germany in 1899 and trained to become a neurologist, specialising in helping people with spinal injuries. When the Nazis came to power in the 1930s, they started to persecute Jewish people. Ludwig tried to help them, defying the law by admitting Jews to hospital even when it had been forbidden. But before long, Ludwig, who was Jewish himself, had to flee the country. In 1939 he escaped to the UK.

In 1944, the British government asked Ludwig to start a National Spinal Injuries Centre at a hospital called Stoke Mandeville. When he arrived for the first time, he was shocked to find many of the patients were left to die from bed sores, pneumonia and infections. At the time, people with spinal injuries were only expected to live for a short while.

Ludwig transformed the place entirely, introducing both new equipment and new ideas for treatment. He made sport a crucial part of therapy, building the confidence and fitness of the paralysed men and women. He hired a sports trainer from the army who started the patients throwing and catching, lifting weights and moving around. Ludwig used staff meetings to encourage the rest of the medics to talk more with their patients.

At first, the hospital directors were unsure about Ludwig's methods, but his results were undeniable. One patient, who had lain on his back for 26 years, was able to walk with the aid of just a stick after six months. The death rate dropped from 80 per cent to 20 per cent within a few years.

In 1948, Ludwig started a wheelchair archery competition in the hospital grounds for 16 people with spinal injuries. The Stoke Mandeville Games grew bigger each year, and disabled athletes from other nations came to compete in many different events. Just 12 years after that first archery competition, Ludwig was invited to the first official Paralympic Games in Rome, Italy, part of the 1960 Olympic Games, with 400 athletes from 23 countries competing. Ludwig's legacy lives on in every Paralympics that has been held since, and all those still to come.

1899-1980

CONSTANTINE

Anti-Racism Cricketer

Learie Constantine was a cricketer who battled against prejudice and ignorance with charm and good humour, relentlessly working to improve race relations in Britain. Connie, as he was nicknamed, was one of the first West Indian athletes to live and regularly compete in the UK in the 1930s.

Connie moved from Trinidad to the UK in 1928 and started playing for Nelson Cricket Club in Lancashire. At first, he and his family were subjected to harsh treatment. They were abused and ignored by those who thought that black people were inferior. Connie sought to dismantle their views and show everyone that people of all skin colours were equal.

As a cricketer, he was highly respected. Connie used his local celebrity to go to public events at cricket clubs in the north of England and tell people about his life. For many, Connie was the first black person they had ever met, and by seeing that he was just like them, they were forced to reconsider their prejudice. Connie was so effective at improving race relations that when the government needed West Indian men to work in Britain during the Second World War, it asked him to help black people settle in places where few people of colour lived. So Connie introduced black workers into factories in Lancashire, ensuring they were made to feel welcome.

But Connie continued to face battles of his own. When he and his family were refused entry to a London hotel in 1943 because they were black, he knew he had to take the owners of the hotel to court. He won the case, and his victory was a turning point in the legal struggle against racism.

After the war, Connie trained to become a lawyer and went into politics both in Trinidad and in the UK. He never stopped fighting racism: in 1963, when a British bus company refused a group of black drivers jobs because of their skin colour, he changed the company owners' minds. His actions helped persuade the government to introduce legislation banning racial discrimination. Connie's refusal to allow prejudice to win transformed the UK for ever.

1901-1971

CHARLES
DREW
Blood Bank Pioneer

Charles was an African American doctor who specialised in how blood works and who revolutionised medicine. When Charles first became a doctor, it wasn't easy to store blood, so transfusions could only take place immediately after a person had donated some. It made it virtually impossible to have a steady supply of blood in all the locations that might need it in cases of emergency.

Charles developed a unique way of separating the blood cells from the liquid part of blood, which is known as plasma. It meant that the plasma would last much longer, and if it was stored correctly in new facilities called blood banks, it could be kept on hand by hospitals until it was needed. The discovery was an astonishing breakthrough.

Not long after Charles invented blood banks, the Second World War broke out in Europe. The fighting led to a vast increase in the demand for blood, so the US government asked Charles to manage a medical campaign called Blood for Britain. In just five months,

Charles and his colleagues collected plasma from over 15,000 people and arranged for it to be shipped to the UK.

When the USA entered the war, Charles was put in charge of a blood bank to be used by American soldiers. He recruited 100,000 people to donate some of their blood, which was then used to save the lives of those wounded on the battlefields. But when the army told Charles that they didn't want blood from African Americans, he felt he had to protest. He knew that there was no difference between the blood of white and black people. The army decided that blood from African Americans could only be donated to soldiers who were African American. Charles believed that this racist policy was not only immoral but put lives at risk too. So when the army refused to change their rules, he resigned.

Charles continued to work as a doctor, but tragically died in a car crash when he was only 45. He was gone too soon, but his legacy lives on each time a person is saved with a blood transfusion, or someone donates blood.

1904-1950

SCHINDLER

Industrialist and Cunning Life-Saver

Oskar Schindler is buried in a Jewish cemetery at Mount Zion in Israel. It may seem odd that a man who was a member of the Nazi Party – a political group that persecuted and murdered millions of Jewish people – should be buried at such a holy site for Jews. But Oskar's story is such a remarkable one that this honour was bestowed upon him.

Oskar became a spy for Nazi Germany in the 1930s when he was out of work. He gave them information about the defences of his homeland, Czechoslovakia, receiving money and gaining their trust in return. But Oskar didn't trust the Nazis, especially their ruthless death squad called the Gestapo.

When the Second World War broke out, Oskar moved to Krakow, in Poland. He took advantage of rules imposed by the Nazi invaders that forbade Jewish people from owning businesses. He bought a Jewish-owned factory producing kitchenware, used his Nazi connections to secure military orders and employed cheap Jewish labour to secure bigger profits. But what happened next is remembered as an extraordinary act of kindness. When the Nazis began rounding up Jewish people in Krakow and sending them to concentration camps, Oskar put his business interests to one side and acted to save them.

Knowing how barbaric the Gestapo was, he began employing more Jews, telling the Nazis they were essential to the war effort. Oskar risked arrest and even execution by doing so, but he knew he was giving his Jewish workers a lifeline. As the tide of the war turned against the Nazis, Oskar convinced them that it would be safer to move his factory to Czechoslovakia. He drew up a list of 1,200 Jewish employees and insisted they travel there with him. He bribed any Nazis who stood in his way.

The plan succeeded, though Oskar's actions left him utterly destitute. When he returned to Germany many years later, the Jewish men, women and children he had saved rallied together to support him financially. After all, they had only survived the horror of the Nazis by being on 'Schindler's List'. They owed him their lives.

1908-1974

'I did what my conscience told me I must do.'

WALLENBERG

Crafty Humanitarian

During the Second World War, Swedish businessman Raoul Wallenberg was sent on a secret mission. The war was devastating Europe, and the Nazis were killing Jews in the countries they invaded. Raoul's task was in Budapest, the capital city of Hungary. The Nazis thought he was there to be a Swedish diplomat, but in truth, he was trying to help Jewish people escape their persecutors.

Raoul knew that time was running out for the Jewish community left in Budapest. Many people had already been rounded up by the Nazis and sent on trains to prison camps. So he leapt into action as soon as he arrived, contacting Jewish families and giving them special travel certificates. The paperwork had no real authority, but Raoul made it look official with stamps, crowns and the official colours of Sweden. He told the Nazis that it guaranteed protection to anyone who held one.

Raoul also used his business and persuasion skills to set up a hospital, nurseries, soup kitchens and safe houses in the city. These places offered Jewish people somewhere to go without fear of arrest, because Raoul put each facility under Swedish diplomatic protection.

On one occasion Raoul even boarded a train which was taking Jews to a death camp. He was carrying a bundle of travel certificates and started to hand them over to the people held captive inside the carriages. He ignored the Nazi guards who fired warning shots above his head and insisted that all those holding paperwork were allowed to get off the train. Raoul and his helpers carried out many such brave deeds. It's estimated that they rescued more than 100,000 Jews by the time the Nazis were forced out of Hungary.

Raoul was arrested by Russian soldiers when the Soviet army liberated Hungary at the end of the war, and he was never released. In 1957, the Soviet government said that he'd died in prison shortly after his arrest, but a number of eyewitnesses reported seeing him in prison years after his supposed death. The circumstances surrounding his final years may never be clear, but we do know it was a tragic end for a man who saved so many lives.

1912-1947

'One person can make a difference.'

SALK

Selfless Scientist

Jonas Salk grew up poor in New York City, USA. He saw the devastating effects that viruses had on communities like his during outbreaks of disease. Where people lived in cramped, dirty conditions, illnesses that could usually be cured would claim the lives of people too poor to afford the right medicine.

Jonas's parents encouraged him to work hard at school, and after achieving excellent results in science he became a scientist, studying the ways that viruses spread. One virus he especially wanted to tackle was polio. Children who caught polio could become so sick that they lost the ability to walk or control their muscles, and could even die.

To try and prevent people from being infected by disease, doctors administer an injection called a vaccine. The vaccine contains enough of the virus to help our bodies practise how to fight off the disease. In Jonas's time, vaccines were still a new idea and they didn't always work. But when they did, it meant the person who developed the vaccine could become very rich by selling it around the world.

Jonas developed a polio vaccine using a sample of the virus. He began testing it in his laboratory, and he even tested it on himself. If he had got his vaccine wrong, he could have given himself polio. But he didn't. Jonas survived, and his vaccine was administered to 1.8 million children as soon as possible.

For many scientists, creating a life-changing medicine would be their ticket to a lifetime of riches. But Jonas did another extraordinary thing. When a journalist asked him who owned the vaccine, he replied, 'The people do'. Because much of his research had been paid for by donations from the public, Jonas was convinced it would be wrong to make millions of dollars for himself from it.

In the year before Jonas created the polio vaccine, there were around 40,000 cases of the disease in the USA. After his vaccine was developed, polio virtually disappeared there and in many other countries. Today, the disease remains extremely rare thanks to Jonas, his groundbreaking vaccine and his decision to give it to the world for free.

1914-1995

MANDELA

Peacebuilding President

Before a schoolteacher renamed him Nelson, Mr Mandela was called Rolihlahla, a word that can mean 'troublemaker'. When he grew up, Nelson certainly caused plenty of trouble for those who ruled South Africa. In doing so, he transformed the lives of millions.

For over 40 years, South Africans were forced to live under Apartheid, a government-enforced system of racial oppression. People were segregated according to their race, and black South Africans weren't allowed to vote and were arrested if they used hospitals, parks or even buses which were labelled 'for whites only'. White people who interacted with black people were punished too. Nelson organised peaceful protests seeking an end to Apartheid, but the police often inflicted brutal violence on the activists. When one demonstration ended in a massacre of 69 black people, Nelson decided non-violent protest wasn't enough. He took command of a group of activists who bombed police stations and government buildings. He was arrested for conspiring to overthrow the state, and sentenced to life in prison. But even though Nelson was beaten and locked in solitary confinement by the guards, he bore them no ill will. Instead, he decided to study their culture and their language, Afrikaans. Nelson believed that by knowing how the rulers of South Africa spoke and thought, he would be able to negotiate with them. He became convinced of the stupidity of violence, and went back to calling for a peaceful end to Apartheid. People began to listen, and many countries stopped trading with South Africa. Under tremendous pressure, the government released Nelson from prison in 1990, after 27 years behind bars.

Once freed, Nelson used his negotiating skills to help bring down Apartheid, and he encouraged black South Africans to forgive their white oppressors. In 1994, in the first election in which black people could vote, Nelson ran for president and won by a landslide. In office, he set up innovative Truth and Reconciliation panels to allow people to voice their anger over the past peacefully. When Nelson died in 2013, the world mourned a man who turned his back on violence and transformed his country through forgiveness.

1918-2013

'Man's goodness is a flame that can be hidden but never extinguished.'

EDMUND

HILLARY

Compassionate Mountaineer

At his school in New Zealand, Edmund was smaller than most of the children his age. He would get barged out of the way when playing sports, and preferred reading instead. He loved stories about adventurers and dreamed of exploring faraway places.

As he grew older and taller, Edmund started to enjoy sports, particularly boxing. When he went on a school trip to Mount Ruapehu, he discovered that his newfound strength and confidence also made him an excellent rock climber. Climbing became his passion, and after leaving school, Edmund went on to conquer the highest mountains in New Zealand and the Swiss Alps. Then he wanted to become the first person to climb to the top of the highest place on Earth, Everest.

Found in the vast mountain range of the Himalayas on the border between China and Nepal, Everest is one of the toughest climbs there is. Edmund set off on his expedition in 1953, helped by local guides called Sherpas. The Sherpa people have spent generations living in the Himalayas, and many of them are

exceptional mountaineers. One of the Sherpas, Tenzing Norgay, climbed with Edmund through the snow and ice to the very top of Everest.

Edmund returned to New Zealand as a celebrity, but he never forgot Nepal and the people who lived there. When he returned to the mountains in 1960, he asked one of the Sherpas, Sirdar Urkien, what he would most like for his people. Urkien replied, 'a school for our village'. Within a year, the school was built, and Edmund devoted himself to assisting the Sherpa people of Nepal for the rest of his life. He set up the Himalayan Trust and built more schools, hospitals, water pipes and even an airstrip. He also arranged for more than 3,000 people to be vaccinated against smallpox.

Today, many places around the world are named after the famous intrepid adventurer Edmund Hillary. But his passion, good nature and love for the people of Nepal mean that his name is especially respected and thought of dearly by those who live in the snowy mountains of the Himalayas.

1919-2008

'Human life is far more important than just getting to the top of a mountain.'

DAVID
ATTENBOROUGH
Documentary Maker and Nature Lover

David's love of animals began as a child, when he collected fossils and cared for newts in a local pond. Since then, his passion for the natural world has made him a hugely popular and respected documentary maker.

When he left the British navy in 1949, David's interest in wildlife and how animals eat, sleep, communicate and survive inspired him to make programmes about them. At first, the TV bosses weren't sure – would anyone want to watch a programme about nature? But David managed to persuade them, and for more than 60 years he has travelled the globe filming wild animals and plants, making people more aware of the incredible nature on Planet Earth. When he started making wildlife films, David also began working hard to support conservation schemes which were groundbreaking at the time, such as nature reserves where animals could be kept safe in their own habitats.

By highlighting the needs of endangered animals and fundraising for sanctuaries and rescue schemes, he has become a figurehead for conservation movements and has helped save some of the world's rarest animals. When he spent time with gorillas in Rwanda in the 1970s, he showed the public how these beautiful creatures were facing extinction.

David's understanding of nature and his calm, gentle approach meant he could film animals and plants close-up, approaching them with curiosity and respect. His programmes allowed people to see creatures in their natural habitats, rather than zoos, for the first time. Viewers became more compassionate towards animals and more concerned about harmful practices such as hunting. Long before people really started to talk about pollution and environmental issues, David was making films which showed the harmful impact some human actions are having upon the creatures we share our planet with.

David's series *Blue Planet II* revealed the true extent of pollution in the world's oceans and sparked a global campaign to stop plastics being discarded into the sea. He may be over 90 years old, but David is still as passionate as ever about the natural world.

B. 1926

'The natural world is the greatest source of so much in life that makes life worth living.'

LUTHER KING JR

Civil Rights Leader

Martin Luther King Jr's role in tackling racism and standing up for civil rights in the USA in the 1950s and 60s earned him a Nobel Peace Prize and the Presidential Medal of Freedom.

Martin grew up at a time when black people weren't allowed to mix with white people or enjoy the same services or rights that white people had. Black children had to attend separate, poorly funded schools, and restaurants and buses had different sections for black and white people to sit in.

Martin experienced this prejudice first-hand when he was just 14. After winning a prize for a speech he'd made about injustice, he climbed aboard the bus home and was forced to give up his seat for a white man. In 1955, when a young black woman named Rosa Parks was arrested for refusing to vacate her seat on a bus in Alabama, it was Martin who led a boycott of the bus company, which gained worldwide attention.

Martin realised that through media coverage and peaceful demonstrations he was able to make racial justice a topic for national debate. He would lead marches of thousands of people across US states where discrimination was in force. Not everyone supported Martin though. Some black Americans believed they should fight back through violence and others pointed out Martin's extramarital affairs. His civil rights protests were met with brutality from white supremacists who didn't believe in equality, and even from police officers.

But little by little, Martin began to change the minds of those ruling the USA, especially when he gave a powerful speech in front of a crowd of 200,000 people and millions more watching on TV. His speech was about his dream of black and white people living together as equals. Laws that banned discrimination, such as the 1964 Civil Rights Act and the 1965 Voting Rights Act, brought that dream a little closer. But on 4 April 1968, just before he was due to speak in support of poorly paid workers, Martin was murdered by a white supremacist. Today that date is a national holiday in the USA, held in honour of a man who sacrificed his life in pursuit of social equality.

1929-1968

'The time is always ripe to do right.'

AGE IS JUST A NUMBER

Crafting clever inventions, devising fundraising schemes and performing random acts of kindness aren't things only adults can do.

Here are some truly amazing kids whose selfless thought for others has helped change lives for the better ...

BARCELONA U14 YOUTH TEAM

B. 2005

In 2016, the under-14 team from Barcelona, Spain, was playing Omiya Ardija of Japan in the finals of a worldwide contest. When the whistle blew, the defeated Omiya players were devastated and broke into tears. The young Barca team stopped celebrating their victory and instead showed their sporting spirit by consoling their opponents.

BOYAN SLAT

B. 1995

In 2011, Dutch 16-year-old Boyan went scuba diving and saw more plastic in the water than fish. It spurred him to start his own company, Ocean Cleanup, and to raise over $30 million to develop a special barrier which gathers up plastic from the oceans to be removed and recycled.

DYLAN MAHALINGAM

B. 1995

When he was nine years old, Dylan began an internet group for young Americans to raise money for local projects. Within 10 years, his Lil' MDG group organised more than three million children around the globe to raise funds to build schools, libraries, playgrounds and community gardens.

IQBAL MASIH

1983–1995

Iqbal was just four years old when he was forced to work in a Pakistan carpet factory. When he escaped, aged 10, he became an activist for child labourers. He helped over 3,000 children to escape slavery before he was tragically assassinated in 1995.

KRTIN NITHIYANANDAM

B. 2000

Aged just 13, Krtin developed a groundbreaking test which has helped doctors detect Alzheimer's disease more quickly. He's still looking for ways to use science for good, and has tackled breast cancer and water conservation so far.

MATTHEW KAPLAN

B. 1997

Matthew was 13 when he discovered that his younger brother was being bullied at school. Matthew responded by starting the Be One Project, which teaches bullies to recognise the pain they cause others and to change their ways. The project is now a national programme throughout the USA.

MOIN YOUNIS

B. 2001

Despite suffering from a disorder which means he has to endure a painful five-hour regime every day to bandage his fragile skin, 17-year-old Moin from Birmingham, UK, still acts as a Young Ambassador for his hospice. He supports other severely ill young people, helps with fundraising and uses social media to launch appeals.

RENE SILVA

B. 1997

Rene launched a newspaper to help the people living in his favela in Rio de Janeiro, Brazil, when he was just 12. He uses it to highlight the problems his community faces and to celebrate the good people who live there. Today, Rene's newspaper has expanded to cover 12 other favelas too.

RICHARD TURERE

B. 1994

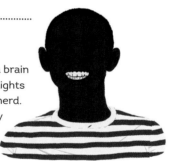

Richard lives in Kenya with his family, tending cattle. When he was nine, he had a brain wave: a system of flashing lights to stop lions attacking his herd. His invention is now used by many other people too, keeping cattle safe and reducing the number of lions killed by farmers.

RYAN WHITE

1971–1990

After being diagnosed with HIV/AIDS at the age of 13, Ryan was banned from school. He courageously campaigned for his right to an education, becoming a spokesperson for those with HIV/AIDS, educating and changing the attitudes of people across the USA before his death in 1990.

Feeling inspired or in awe of the achievements of these good guys? Why not join them?

Perhaps you have an idea for a fundraising initiative or a kind deed you could perform to bring a little bit of good into the world.

HOLLOWS

Ophthalmologist and Aid Pioneer

Fred was born in Dunedin, New Zealand. He was always a helpful chap. As a student, he carried a heavy backpack for the mountaineer Edmund Hillary, a kind act that the climber never forgot. But it is his dedication to the world's poorest people that has had the most significant impact. You really could say that Fred was a man of vision.

As an ophthalmologist in Sydney, Australia, in the 1960s, Fred would treat people's sight problems on a daily basis. One day, he treated two elderly Aboriginal Australian men from a remote village in the desert called Wattie Creek. The men were almost blind because of an eye condition that wasn't thought to exist in Australia at the time. When Fred visited Wattie Creek with the two men, he discovered to his horror that many more villagers had the same terrible eye illness. The Aboriginal Australians didn't have the sort of access to health care that wealthier Australians enjoyed, so Fred began to treat them for free.

Fred understood that the severe eye problems in the villages were linked to the poverty he saw there, and he knew that there were plenty of other places with similar issues. So as well as working to improve healthcare services for aboriginal peoples, he also began to visit impoverished communities in Africa and Asia. Fred couldn't treat everybody on his own, so he established the Fred Hollows Foundation, which trained local eye doctors and set up factories and clinics in countries such as Ethiopia and Afghanistan, to make special lenses to restore people's eyesight. One place that needed aid was Nepal. Fred's old friend Edmund had become world-famous by climbing mountains there, and he returned the favour from all those years ago by helping him to set up eye-care clinics.

Fred believed that preventing blindness and reducing the cost of health care for the poor was his mission in life. Even when he became seriously ill himself, he left his hospital bed to go to Vietnam and teach 300 doctors how to treat blindness. Today, the foundation he created continues to save the sight of millions of people around the world.

1929–1993

HARVEY
MILK

Gay Rights Activist

'Rights are won only by those who make their voices heard,' said Harvey Milk. But for years, Harvey, like many gay men and women, was scared to speak up. He was living in the USA in the 1960s, a time when the law was used to treat gay people differently from everyone else. They could be arrested and imprisoned just because of their sexuality.

Many people, including Harvey, feared that they would be dismissed from their jobs if their employers found out that they were gay, so they kept it a secret. But in the 1960s, some Americans began to protest against the laws that persecuted people for being gay. At first, Harvey just joined in the parades and demonstrations. But he soon became known as a determined campaigner and activist who brought the gay community together, gave it a powerful voice and made politicians take notice of its anger and desire for change.

After leading boycotts of companies which had banned employees from being openly gay, Harvey realised that the best way to ensure that the law treated everyone fairly regardless of their sexuality was for him to get elected as a politician.

So from the little camera shop that he ran in Castro Street in San Francisco, he campaigned to become a member of the local government. Harvey wanted to fight for the rights of everyone in his community, not just gay people. He succeeded in being one of the first openly gay men elected to public office in the USA, and worked hard to improve housing and childcare for local families.

Harvey's campaign had a huge impact on the attitudes of many American people, but not all. One rival politician, Dan White, took a gun to Harvey's office in 1978 and shot him dead. The community was shocked to its core and thousands marched to City Hall in a silent vigil to remember Harvey. The killer was convicted, but he received a light sentence and only served six years in prison. Nevertheless, Harvey's bravery inspired gay men and women to hold their heads high and demand equality. His election was groundbreaking, and he changed attitudes across the country.

1930–1978

'Hope will never be silent.'

GORBACHEV

Liberating Politician

Mikhail Gorbachev was the leader of the Communist Party which ruled Russia and its surrounding states as a colossal superpower called the Soviet Union. When he was appointed in 1985, Western countries such as the USA and Britain were locked in a 'Cold War' with the Soviet Union and had been since the end of the Second World War. The two sides didn't fight battles directly, but created deadly nuclear weapons to threaten each other with the prospect of war. The stand-off left Europe split in two across a heavily fortified border.

The leaders of the Soviet Union had often used terror and repression to keep order in the countries they governed. They pretended to be democratic, but only one candidate was put forward for each election, so voters had no real choice. Newspapers weren't allowed to report bad news, most popular Western music was banned and shopping for food meant hours of waiting in long queues for basics such as bread and cheese. After 40 years of isolation, the Soviet Union was struggling to feed its people.

When Mikhail became leader, he bravely sought to change the Soviet Union. He wanted citizens to be able to speak more openly and vote in real elections. He believed that spending less on weapons would mean more money for improving people's living standards. So, Mikhail sought to end the Cold War with Western countries. He met with US President Ronald Reagan in 1987 and they each agreed to destroy all of their short and medium-range missiles. By granting new freedoms to the people of the Soviet Union and ending the arms race, Mikhail became celebrated as a peacemaker.

But the changes in living standards he'd hoped for were too slow in coming for people enjoying their new freedom. In Eastern Europe and parts of the Soviet Union, people took to the streets, tearing down borders with the West and using the democratic rights that Mikhail had given them to call for an end to Soviet rule. Finally, the Cold War was over, a 40-year-long period of fear and uncertainty for millions worldwide. In thanks, Mikhail was awarded the Nobel Peace Prize.

B. 1931

JOSÉ
MUJICA

Humble President

When José Mujica became president of Uruguay in 2010, he was unlike anyone else to have held such high office. Instead of living in a luxurious presidential building in the capital city Montevideo, José continued to live at home on his small farm where he grew and sold flowers, with his wife Lucía and his three-legged dog, Manuela.

He also refused to be driven around by a chauffeur in a government limousine, instead preferring to drive to political meetings in his beaten-up old car. José would often stop and give hitch-hikers a ride into the city, surprising them when they realised that the plainly dressed man driving the rattling car was the president of their country. José wasn't wealthy, but he still donated 90 per cent of his salary to charities. 'You don't stop being a common man just because you are president,' he said when asked why he didn't live like other world leaders.

His desire to help the poorest people in his country stemmed from his childhood. José came from a very deprived part of Uruguay where people struggled to survive. As a young man, he blamed the country's cruel military leaders for the widespread poverty and so joined a violent revolutionary group that was trying to bring about change. But he was captured and spent 13 years in prison.

After his release, José decided it would be wiser to use peaceful ways of helping people. He became a campaigner and politician, and his humble manner and simple lifestyle made him very popular with the people of Uruguay. When he was elected to become president, he promised to make changes to the social justice, education and welfare systems in his country to help the poor.

José became so famous he was even offered $1 million for his old car, but wealth didn't interest him at all. 'All I do is live like the majority of my people, not the minority,' he said, declining the offer. When his term of office as president came to an end, he'd achieved many of his aims, uniting the people of Uruguay into a strong community. José stepped down to return to his farm for good.

B. 1935

14TH DALAI LAMA

Spiritual Leader and Human Rights Activist

When he was just two years old, Tenzin was found by monks and proclaimed to be the fourteenth Dalai Lama, the spiritual leader of a land called Tibet. Buddhists teach that when a person dies, their spirit is reincarnated in the body of someone else. The Buddhists of Tibet believe that Tenzin is the latest reincarnation of the Dalai Lama, a spiritual leader filled with compassion for humankind.

When you imagine a monk, you might think of an earnest, quiet man. But Tenzin is often very playful when he speaks, frequently punctuating his arguments with jokes, even during talks on grave topics. He likes to have fun with audiences.

Tenzin is world-famous for leading the people of Tibet in a struggle for independence from China. He was only a teenager when the Chinese army invaded his homeland. As the Dalai Lama, he went to China to meet with the military leaders, hoping to negotiate a withdrawal. But the Chinese refused and began to imprison and even kill some Tibetans. Tenzin was forced to escape from Tibet with thousands of others. They have lived in exile in Dharamshala, India,

ever since, keeping up a non-violent struggle for independence. Tenzin talks to world leaders to highlight the plight of his people and campaign for change, whilst also being a passionate defender of people who have fallen victim to human rights abuses elsewhere in the world.

One of the causes close to Tenzin's heart is climate change, especially in Tibet. There are so many glaciers in the Himalayan mountain range that forms part of Tibet that it is called the 'Third Pole'. But the glaciers are melting due to rising temperatures across the planet. Tenzin often warns global leaders of the catastrophic consequences this could have upon the rivers which flow through villages, towns and cities across Asia.

By championing human rights for all, Tenzin has become a spiritual leader whose word is respected by people from many backgrounds and religions. The young boy who was plucked from a mountain village has grown into a beacon of hope for many, and in 1989 he was awarded the Nobel Peace Prize for his human rights advocacy.

B. 1935

JAMES
HARRISON

Blood Donor and Life Saver

To say that James Harrison is a giving kind of guy is quite an understatement. For over 60 years, James has been regularly attending blood donation sessions at his local hospital in New South Wales, Australia.

Millions of people around the world donate their blood to help keep others alive when they suffer an injury or become unwell. What makes James's story so special is that his blood is, well, rather special too. When he was 14, James had surgery to remove one of his lungs. As part of his recovery, he received 13 litres of donated blood to help him get better. It didn't take long for James to decide that he wanted to donate his own blood regularly in return, as a means of saying thank you to those who had given theirs to save him. And James has been as good as his word – because since he turned 18, he has donated blood on around 1,200 occasions. That means he attends a donation clinic almost once a week!

After a few donations, the hospital discovered that James's medical treatment had altered the plasma in his blood into a unique type that is full of potent antibodies which can help humans battle certain diseases. At the same time, doctors were struggling to treat a condition called rhesus disease, which affects pregnant women and can result in the death of newborn babies. Scientists were desperate to come up with a solution, and thanks to James's blood donations, they did.

By using his plasma to develop a medicine for the immune system, doctors could give pregnant women who were at risk of carrying rhesus disease an injection to stop the condition from affecting their baby. Since that scientific breakthrough, it's been estimated that James's blood alone has saved the lives of 2.4 million babies.

James was recognised in 2003 with the Guinness World Record for the most blood ever donated by one person, and he has been awarded the Medal of the Order of Australia for inspiring others to donate too. One of the people he inspired was his grandson, who gave blood for the first time on his sixteenth birthday, as soon as he was legally allowed to.

B. 1936

PATRICK
STEWART
Actor and Campaigner

Patrick is a British actor who has appeared in a wealth of movies including the X-Men franchise, in which he plays Professor Charles Xavier. Before that, he became famous on TV in the role of Captain Jean-Luc Picard in *Star Trek: The Next Generation*. But Patrick is also well known as a strident campaigner who raises awareness of topics that many people have trouble even discussing.

Patrick uses his fame to talk about his childhood experiences growing up in a home where domestic violence – when one partner in a relationship harms the other – was common. When he was young, he witnessed repeated violence by his father towards his mother.

Many victims of domestic abuse are often too afraid to speak up or ask for help. They can feel ashamed, and worry about being judged, and may fear that going to the police will only make matters worse. As a result, much domestic violence happens behind closed doors and in secret. When Patrick discusses his childhood, he raises awareness of domestic abuse, making it clear that violence against

women is never acceptable, and that victims are never responsible for their suffering. He is a patron of Refuge, a British charity which supports women experiencing and recovering from domestic violence.

Patrick's dad fought in battles during the Second World War, and when the war ended, he struggled to cope with life away from the army. Long after his father died, Patrick discovered that he had suffered from a psychological condition called post-traumatic stress disorder, or PTSD, caused by the pressures of wartime combat. Experts today think this had probably been one of the reasons for his violent behaviour. So although Patrick wasn't able to help his father deal with his PTSD during his lifetime, today he campaigns to raise awareness of the condition among former soldiers and their families, helping them to get treatment.

The various characters that Patrick has played on stage and on screen have brought him much acclaim. But it is his role of activist and campaigner that Patrick is most proud of.

B. 1940

MUHAMMAD
ALI
Boxer and Humanitarian

Arguably the most famous sportsman who ever lived, Muhammad Ali was born in Kentucky, USA, in 1942. A three-time heavyweight champion, he wasn't shy about letting people know how talented a boxer he was. Muhammad would use poetry to belittle his opponents while his catchphrase, 'I am the Greatest', led some people to call him arrogant. But beneath the punching and the trash-talk was a compassionate humanitarian who should be remembered as much for his kindness as for his world titles.

Muhammad's caring side came to light when he decided not to serve in the US army during the Vietnam War. 'I ain't got no quarrel with them Vietcong', he insisted. But it was the law for young men to join the army at the time, and Muhammad paid a high price for refusing to go to war. He was sentenced to prison, fined, stripped of the titles he'd won and banned from boxing for three years in his prime.

During the ban, he spent his time trying to change society for the better. He toured colleges and universities using his skills as an inspirational speaker to discuss the war and racial inequality in the USA. Many who heard him began to question these things too; Muhammad's bravery encouraged Martin Luther King Jr to publicly condemn the war.

Muhammad was a formidable fighter in the ring, but he also showed great compassion towards his opponents. When one of the few boxers to have beaten him, Ken Norton, woke up in hospital after a near-death car crash, he found Muhammad at his bedside in prayer.

After his retirement from boxing, Muhammad devoted his life to charitable work, even as he suffered from Parkinson's disease which eventually robbed him of the ability to speak. He helped to deliver medical aid and food to hungry children around the world, and even travelled to Iraq to personally secure the release of 15 American hostages during the Gulf War. Muhammad's activism was recognised internationally, and in the years before his death he was named a Messenger of Peace by the UN and awarded the Presidential Medal of Freedom by George W. Bush.

1942-2016

'Service to others is the rent you pay for your room here on Earth.'

KI-MOON

Softly Spoken Secretary-General

Ki-moon grew up during a civil war which split his homeland of Korea into two separate nations: North Korea and South Korea. When the fighting stopped, he watched as peacekeeping troops from the United Nations (UN) helped South Korea to recover and rebuild. It left a strong impression.

As an adult, Ki-moon served as a negotiator and ambassador for South Korea. He became known for his quiet and respectful personality, beneath which lay strong perseverance. It wasn't long before he was appointed Secretary-General of the UN in 2007.

Leading the UN is a challenging job, involving trying to persuade countries with different politics, cultures and personalities to reach agreements. Ki-moon decided that one of the best ways he could help was to visit war-torn countries such as Myanmar, Ukraine and Somalia, often being the first UN chief to do so. Ki-moon met with leaders in Sudan and persuaded them to allow Blue Helmets – the UN's peacekeeping troops – into the Darfur region. Darfur had become a war zone, but Ki-moon's intervention meant that the Blue Helmets could finally deliver aid and food supplies to thousands of trapped refugees. Ki-moon also stood up for gay rights, condemning governments which persecute gay people and becoming the first UN chief to appoint someone to oversee gay rights. It was a brave stance, because many countries of the UN had pressured him to stay silent.

But his most important mission was about climate change. He knew it was essential that every country agreed to limit global warming, and he brought together global leaders to sign a groundbreaking pledge called the Paris Agreement. 'We do not have any Plan B, because we do not have Planet B', he said.

Some people criticised Ki-moon for his leadership style – they said he was too quiet. But not everyone can grab the spotlight, and Ki-moon's calm approach and understanding nature were rooted in the teachings of Confucius. He helped to build bridges between warring factions and bring much-needed aid to victims of disasters around the world.

B. 1944

CHRISTOPHER
REEVE

Actor and Superman

Just like the comic book superhero that he was most famous for playing, Christopher led two lives. As an actor, he brought Superman to the movie screen in the 1970s and 80s. Tall, handsome and athletic, he was the perfect man to play Clark Kent, an ordinary news reporter who transforms into a gallant superhero. Away from the screen, Christopher supported charities such as Save the Children. He also demonstrated against human rights abuses in the USA and in Chile, coming to the support of people who were being persecuted for disagreeing with the government.

But Christopher's life changed in 1995 when the horse he was riding threw him off. The accident damaged his spine so severely it meant he would spend the rest of his life in a wheelchair. But Christopher was determined that being paralysed would never stop him acting or campaigning.

Just months after his terrible accident, Christopher appeared on stage at the Oscars to introduce an award. Many of his fellow actors, and millions of TV viewers, were shocked to see him in a wheelchair and breathing with the aid of a ventilator, but Christopher showed the world that he was not going to let paralysis stop him. He later said the appearance gave him the confidence to continue making films, many of which were about confronting difficult topics.

Three years later, Christopher made another important appearance, this time in front of the US Senate. He called for more money to improve the lives of paralysed people and to fund scientific research that might help some of them to walk again. In fact, Christopher campaigned vigorously for the rest of his life, championing new studies into the treatment of paralysis even as his own health gradually deteriorated.

He died aged only 52, but his legacy as a true superman lives on. The Christopher and Dana Reeve Foundation has raised over $100 million, funding everything from research laboratories and specialised clinics to carers and equipment for people with paralysis.

1952-2004

BERNERS-LEE

World Wide Web Warrior

Today we browse the web without a thought. But it's all thanks to a British computer engineer, Tim Berners-Lee, and his incredible act of generosity, that we have the World Wide Web at our fingertips.

Tim seemed destined to do something clever with computers. When he was a child, he learned all about electronics from toy trains, and at university he built a computer using an old TV. He was a genius with technology, but he wasn't good at remembering people's names or snippets of information. So when Tim started working at a lab, he wrote some software to help his memory. Scientists would ask him for information and the software would enable him to click on certain words that linked to a database with the answers.

Then Tim came up with the idea of sharing information using a network of connected computers, and he began designing better software to make it happen. He drew a diagram to show how the interconnecting databases might work. It looked like a spider's web, so his plan was called the World Wide Web.

But by the early 1990s, other companies had similar ideas and Tim faced a tough choice. Should he get an exclusive licence, called a patent, for his web software and charge people to use it? Or should he make it available for everyone to use for free?

Patenting his web could have made Tim a billionaire. But instead, he chose to upload the software on to the internet for free. He felt that his creation could bring people together – enabling families, businesses and other groups to communicate more, to share and support each other. Sure enough, once the web was online, people around the world started creating websites, searching for information, buying and selling, finding new friends, contacting old ones and much more.

Over half of the world's population – 3.8 billion people – use the World Wide Web today. It's still free to use, and Tim is determined to keep it that way. In 2009 he founded the World Wide Web Foundation to fight for digital equality – for the right of everyone to access the web and use it to improve their lives.

B. 1955

BILL
GATES
Generous Entrepreneur

As a child, Bill loved to read books. He'd spend hours with his head in an encyclopaedia learning about science and the world around him – to the point where eventually Bill's exasperated parents had to ban him from reading at the dinner table. But his love of books and science certainly paid off. After spending hours in the computer lab together, Bill and his school friend Paul Allen decided to set up a software company when they were only 20 years old. In 1975, people were just beginning to use computers at work and home for the first time, and Bill and Paul used innovation and keen business skills to build their company into the biggest tech company in the world: Microsoft.

Microsoft got so successful that Bill became extremely rich – in fact, for a long time, he was the richest person on the planet. But he knew that he didn't need all that wealth, so he and his wife established the Bill and Melinda Gates Foundation to fight diseases such as malaria and HIV/AIDS. Bill pledged to devote the bulk of his money to the foundation and has donated $28 billion of his fortune so far.

He has also convinced other very wealthy people to pledge billions of dollars for charity. In 2010, Bill and Melinda teamed up with businessman Warren Buffett to launch the Giving Pledge, an invitation to billionaires around the world to promise to give away more than half of their wealth to good causes. As many as 175 have signed up so far, transforming the way that the super-rich think about donating to charity. In 2006, Bill announced he was resigning from his job at Microsoft to work full time for his foundation. His aims are ambitious: the foundation's vaccination programme has cut the measles death rate in Africa by 74 per cent. Bill also announced his mission to wipe out polio, continuing the pioneering work of Jonas Salk – today it has been almost entirely eradicated.

By demonstrating how the world's richest man can help millions of the poor, Bill has led a new wave of philanthropists – wealthy individuals who pledge their money to help others – to do the same. His vision to transform the world with kindness has set an example to the super-wealthy for years to come.

B. 1955

A I
WEIWEI
Activist Artist

Weiwei is an artist who has spoken out against human rights abuse, especially when committed by the government of his homeland, China. His masterpieces include everything from films and sculptures to buildings; Weiwei first became known to many people outside China when he helped to design the famous Bird's Nest stadium for the 2008 Beijing Olympics.

But when his design was praised around the world, Weiwei used this public platform to speak out against the government of China when an earthquake struck in the Sichuan province. The quake destroyed countless classrooms, many of which had been built by the government with cheap, shoddy materials, and thousands of children died. The Chinese politicians didn't want to reveal how many, but Weiwei set up a blog and asked for volunteers to help him find out the truth. In 2009, Weiwei unveiled a new piece of art: he had covered a German museum's facade with a quote from the mother of one of the victims: 'All I want is to let the world remember she had been living happily for seven years.'

It wasn't long before Weiwei was attacked by police officers and imprisoned. Criticising the government had landed Weiwei in big trouble. Ironically, he was tortured for condemning the cruelty of the country's leaders. The injuries caused his brain to swell dangerously, but when he recovered, Weiwei used the medical scan of his brain to create a protest artwork.

In 2010, Weiwei created his most famous work at the Tate Modern gallery in London, UK, filling the exhibition hall with a carpet of around 100 million porcelain sunflower seeds. Weiwei wanted to show that each seed was individual and unique, but collectively, they were powerful – just as the voices of individuals can be powerful when they shout together. The artwork means something else too. Weiwei remembers the violent Cultural Revolution that took place in China when he was 10 years old. It was a time of poverty and uncertainty, but when he thinks of that time, he thinks of the sunflower-seed snacks that people shared with one another, and the kindnesses and friendships that he witnessed during that difficult time.

B. 1957

OBAMA

Fun-Loving President

Twice elected the president of the USA, Barack Obama has been called 'the kindest man to grace the Oval Office'. Along with having many thoughtful government policies, such as more affordable health care and better management of the environment, Barack was admired around the world for his friendly, down-to-earth approach to the presidency.

Barack worked as a community organiser for many years, helping people living on low incomes in tough housing estates in Chicago to get better opportunities and support. Many presidents are born into wealthy families and are expected to become politicians, but Barack worked his way up from the bottom. So when he ran for president, his campaign slogan 'Yes We Can!' inspired voters to believe that the USA could become fairer for all. In 2008, Barack became the first black US president.

Having experienced racism throughout his life, Barack cared passionately about creating a world that was more equal. He enacted policies to help young people afford university education even if they were poor, and he made it illegal to discriminate against gay men and women. Barack also proudly called himself a feminist. He supported his wife Michelle, a talented lawyer, as she campaigned for healthier lifestyles to tackle childhood obesity, and he championed his daughters Sasha and Malia to succeed in school and beyond.

Barack would always welcome everyone – from young children dressed as Spiderman to a 106-year-old woman – to the White House with the same courtesy he showed kings, queens and world leaders. He had plenty of serious business to get on with, but Barack was also known for his sense of fun, even stopping meetings to dance with guests and staff.

Not all of Barack's policies were popular; his use of drone rockets to bomb nations in conflict with the USA angered people, for example. But he won many friends around the world with his humility and sincere ambition to change the world for the better. And by setting an example, he showed millions of children that whatever their background, it was possible for them to lead their country.

B. 1961

'It is
absolutely
men's
responsibility
to fight
sexism too.'

MICHAEL

Pop Star and Secret Philanthropist

George Michael was a global pop star with hit records and sell-out concerts. But after his sudden death in 2016, it became apparent that he would be remembered for his many undercover acts of kindness.

George spent his adult life in the public spotlight, and he often appeared in the media because of things he'd done wrong. He led a troubled life, struggling to cope with an addiction to drugs. But George's unique voice and compelling songwriting won him many fans. In 1984, his band Wham! donated all the royalties from their hit single *Last Christmas* to charity, and he performed at a concert called Live Aid the following year, helping to raise millions of pounds for starving families in Ethiopia.

George used his platform to support plenty of other causes too. He supported charities for those living with AIDS and campaigned for the rights of gay men and women. He also performed concerts for free to raise money for the nurses who'd looked after his dying mum. However, George conducted many of his good deeds in utmost secrecy. After his death, people came forward to share stories of how he'd changed lives for the better. For instance, George worked anonymously as a volunteer at a shelter for the homeless, and he set up a little-known trust to support disabled people.

George's fame and success brought him great wealth, and he frequently shared it with people in need. He once helped a student nurse who was working part-time in a restaurant by tipping her £5,000 so she could pay off her student debt. And he anonymously gave thousands of pounds to two women he'd seen on TV who needed expensive medical treatment. When one of his songs topped the charts, he donated all of the proceeds to a children's charity, Childline. After his death, the charity's founder revealed that George had given millions of pounds to them over the years, but had always insisted that his donations be kept secret. George has become a role model for those who believe in doing good to help others – rather than simply to enhance your own reputation.

1963-2016

'Nurses, doctors, teachers: those are the people who deserve the credit.'

MUSK

Space-Age Entrepreneur

As a child growing up in South Africa, Elon Musk loved reading science fiction. He would daydream about the future and become so distracted that his teachers thought he was deaf because he didn't answer their questions. But this fascination with the future has made him one of the most exciting businessmen of his age.

When he turned 17, Elon was expected to serve in the South African army, a legal requirement for all white men at the time. But back then, the government wanted its soldiers to carry out oppressive, racist laws that Elon hated, so he refused and relocated to Canada. Once there, he put his love of science fiction and gadgets to use by starting technology businesses such as PayPal, which he later sold to become hugely wealthy.

With billions of dollars in the bank, Elon started to make his sci-fi fantasies become a reality. He was most anxious about climate change; he knew that as humankind filled the planet with more cars and power stations, pollution would cause the Earth to heat up.

The changes to our planet could be catastrophic, from newly formed deserts to widespread flooding and natural disasters like hurricanes and tornadoes.

Elon has dedicated his career to finding ways to help us survive. His first move was to found a company called Tesla to develop cars that weren't reliant on fossil fuels. Elon has also helped to devise new types of affordable solar panels so that more people can harness clean energy in their homes and offices. He's even developing high-speed underground transportation routes that will be more environmentally friendly than cars on roads.

But Elon's ambitions don't stop there. He thinks that one day, Earth won't be able to sustain all of us, and is working on ambitious plans to send people to live on Mars instead. His SpaceX rockets are intended to get us to the red planet. And some people think that the young entrepreneur is crazy for dreaming up such a plan. But Elon disagrees. He says, 'When something is important enough, you do it even if the odds are not in your favour.'

B. 1971

OLIVER

Chef and Food Revolutionary

Jamie's appreciation of how food can bring people together began as he helped in the kitchen of his parents' restaurant in Essex, in the south of the UK. In the late 1990s, he became famous as a TV chef who made cooking fast and fun. But he doesn't just teach us how to cook. Jamie passionately believes that food can change lives for the better.

In 2002, Jamie launched a restaurant group called Fifteen, which hires unemployed young people from disadvantaged backgrounds. Through Fifteen, Jamie has taught hundreds of people the skills they need to work in a professional kitchen and eventually to run their own restaurants.

Jamie is also concerned about our over-reliance on junk food, and how it's impacting on our health – particularly children's. For over 10 years, he has pressured governments to make school dinners more nutritious and free to those most in need of it. When his TV show highlighted the sorts of meals children were eating at school, including dishes such as Turkey Twizzlers filled with salt and fat, it led to wholesale changes in school dinners. Ever since, lunchtime menus across the UK have included more fruit and vegetables and less processed food.

Jamie has also led protests to reduce the amount of sugar found in foods. In 2017, after many years of calling for a tax on sugary drinks, he successfully persuaded the British government to introduce one to tackle rising rates of obesity. It's led to many soft drinks companies changing their recipes to make them less sugary.

In 2010, he set up the Jamie Oliver Food Foundation in an effort to spark a global food revolution. When Jamie took his *Ministry of Food* programme to Australia to teach people how to cook nutritious meals from scratch, he transformed the lives of many, encouraging them to eat more vegetables and spend less on unhealthy takeaway meals. He's been awarded an MBE from the Queen for tackling health issues and childhood obesity, but Jamie isn't ready to stop yet – there's too much work still to be done!

B. 1975

CUMBERBATCH

Actor and Campaigner

Benedict Cumberbatch is the actor who really makes it cool to be kind. Famous for playing the detective Sherlock Holmes and the magical superhero Doctor Strange, Benedict is also well known for his many acts of compassion in real life.

The son of two actors, Benedict was born in Kensington and Chelsea in London, one of the wealthiest areas of Britain. He spent his childhood at a private boarding school with kids from similarly privileged backgrounds. So it's fair to say that Benedict has been very lucky, but rather than take this for granted, he has chosen to advocate for people who are less fortunate than him.

Among many other issues, he's campaigned for humanitarian causes, women's rights and charities supporting people with cancer. His activism has often been inspired by the roles he plays. After playing the part of Professor Stephen Hawking in a TV drama, who spent much of his life in a wheelchair because of his motor neurone disease (MND), Benedict became a patron of the MND Association.

He also spoke out on behalf of gay men and women after he played the part of a war hero named Alan Turing, who was persecuted for his sexuality in the 1950s.

Benedict has even been known to start a campaign on the stage. When the civil war in Syria forced many people to flee and take dangerous boat trips across the sea to Europe, Benedict wanted to help. At the time, he was appearing in a play in front of hundreds of people each night, and as the refugee crisis unfolded, he appealed to the audience at the end of each performance to ask them for donations for the refugees. He raised over £150,000 through this simple act. Benedict's passion for acting has also led him to support disadvantaged children who dream of becoming artists and performers.

When asked about the many causes he contributes to, Benedict is strikingly modest. 'I feel very strongly about the little work I do when I have the time', he says. But the so-called 'little' work he refers to has had a truly big impact.

B. 1976

GREEN

Author & Vlogger

John is an author whose novels such as *Looking for Alaska* and *Paper Towns* have guided a generation of teenagers and young adults through friendship and heartache. He was a shy child who was often bullied, and his books reflect his experiences growing up with anxiety issues. He deals openly with the harsh realities that teenagers face and talks to readers in a non-patronising way.

But along with writing bestselling books, John also hosts a video blog. He started out posting a daily vlog to his brother, Hank, on YouTube so they could stay in touch. They discussed everything from science to books, fast food to sports. Just like John's books, the vlogs soon became extremely popular and he began to use them to build a community of fans, known as Nerdfighters, who shared his vision of making the world a better place.

John created Project for Awesome in 2007, an annual initiative where thousands of people post vlogs letting the world know about good causes that need help and support. The Nerdfighter community promotes the videos and fundraises for the charities, and as a result, Project For Awesome has raised millions for worthy causes since it first began.

It was through the Nerdfighter community that John first came to know Esther Earl, a teenage girl with terminal cancer. Esther became an inspirational vlogger and John helped to secure a grant for her treatment and share her videos widely. When Esther died aged just 16, John wrote *The Fault in Our Stars* about a young girl with cancer in her honour. It became the most successful book he'd ever written, and before long, a blockbuster movie based on the book was released.

John's experience of being bullied at school inspired him to create Be Internet Awesome. This online project uses vlogs to teach kids, teachers and parents about digital citizenship and how to be kind to each other when communicating online, as well as working to combat cyber-bullying. It's another example of what makes John unique: he looks at the internet and sees it as a tool that can be harnessed for good.

B. 1977

DROGBA

Footballer and Peacekeeper

D idier was born in Abidjan, a city in Côte d'Ivoire, a small nation on the west coast of Africa. As a child, he would play football all day long in a local car park, and when his parents both lost their jobs and the family moved to France, Didier joined a local amateur team called Levallois. He was a great goal-scorer, and before long he was scouted to play for top European teams like Marseille and Chelsea. Didier has helped his clubs to many title wins in his career, including the FA Cup, Premier League and Champions League.

When Côte d'Ivoire's national team qualified for the World Cup for the first time ever in 2006, Didier played a crucial role. For Côte d'Ivoire, one of Africa's smaller nations, to reach the tournament was a tremendous achievement. The whole country was proud of Didier and his teammates. And the country's pride shot through the roof when Didier's goals helped Côte d'Ivoire reach the World Cup again in 2010 and 2014.

Off the pitch, Didier uses his wealth and fame to assist the people of Côte d'Ivoire and other African nations as much as he can. For example, when he received a £3 million sponsorship deal, he donated the cash to fund a new hospital in Abidjan. And he took part in exhibition matches to raise awareness and money for people suffering from a terrible disease called Ebola, which spread through parts of Africa in 2014, killing thousands.

Didier even managed to help bring a civil war to an end – quite a feat for a footballer! For five years, two armies had fought in a conflict in Côte d'Ivoire that had claimed thousands of lives. Didier realised that soldiers on both sides were massive football fans, and as his country's most famous sports star, in 2006 he made a television appeal for them to lay down their weapons.

Such was the respect that the warring sides had for Didier that they did exactly that. He became a Goodwill Ambassador for the United Nations and participated in the formal peace process by joining his country's Truth and Reconciliation panel, helping Côte d'Ivoire to heal the wounds of war.

B. 1978

GREEN

Rapper and Mental Health Campaigner

. . . .

Professor Green is the stage name of the British rap artist Stephen Manderson, famous for his award-winning songs filled with honest lyrics that reflect his feelings about his upbringing. But since 2015, Stephen has also been a documentary filmmaker and mental health campaigner.

Stephen talks about his own difficult childhood to inspire others to come to terms with their experiences. He grew up on a tough council estate in Hackney, east London. His mum left the family when he was a baby and his dad struggled to cope, eventually taking his own life. As he grew older, Stephen found a way of dealing with the loss of his father and understanding his emotions through music.

Through TV shows and other media, Stephen has encouraged boys and men to speak openly about mental health issues. For many men, the thought of discussing their emotions is scary. Stephen is leading the way to change that attitude. By revealing how he feels about his father's suicide and the impact it has had on his own life, Stephen encourages other boys and men to do the same. He talks about how, as a child, he was unable to interact with other children or feel happiness the same way they did. By discussing his feelings of abandonment and loneliness, he has been able to connect with many people who have experienced similar situations and emotions.

Instead of basking in his stardom, Stephen speaks at help centres and in campaigns for Calm, a charity working to prevent male suicide. In doing so, he has given many people hope and inspiration. His filmmaking has also investigated the links between growing up in poverty and its impact on the mental health of young people.

Stephen's bravery in speaking up and speaking out about his childhood experiences has been a massive comfort for people who are struggling to express painful emotions, and has helped spark a change in attitudes about how boys and men should be expected to deal with difficult circumstances.

. . . .

B. 1983

USAIN

BOLT

Athlete Who Remembers His Roots

Usain Bolt didn't just rise from a humble background in Jamaica to become the world's fastest man. He also became a very generous one. In fact, he even got himself in trouble for donating money to those in need.

Usain grew up in a poor Jamaican village called Sherwood Content. There was no running water or electricity there, but that didn't stop Usain from playing sports, particularly cricket. The skills he practised on those streets helped turn him into a world-class athlete! And when he finally became a gold-medal-winning sprinter for the Jamaican team, touring the world and breaking records at Olympic Games, Usain didn't forget his homeland. Whenever sponsors approached him to appear in adverts, he insisted they were always filmed in Jamaica so that local people could feature as extras and the Jamaican economy would benefit.

It was just one of the many ways in which Usain has given back to his nation and community. He also paid for a new sewage system, running water and electricity in Sherwood Content. When he heard that his old school might have to close its sports clubs, he donated $1.3 million to keep them open, as well as new equipment including 50 pairs of football boots. Usain even used to make a habit of giving away $30,000 to strangers each December. But a few years ago, the Jamaican police asked him to stop handing out money because it was causing fights among the crowds who came to see him. So, determined to help out as much as he could, he set up a charity, the Usain Bolt Foundation, which provides money for underprivileged kids in Jamaica and beyond.

On the track, Usain gained the admiration of fans and fellow athletes for his friendliness – he even stopped a live TV interview during the 2012 Olympics so that he could stand in silence to pay respect to the national anthem of Jamaica's athletics rivals, the USA.

As an athlete, Usain became a hero who Jamaicans were proud of. But he continues to be a role model for millions thanks to his good deeds, even now he has retired.

B. 1986

'I was always taught that the fortunate help the not-so-fortunate.'

KAEPERNICK

American Footballer

In 2012, American football quarterback Colin Kaepernick led his team, the San Francisco 49ers, to the National Football League (NFL) Super Bowl. Reaching the Super Bowl is a crowning moment in an NFL player's career and Colin's efforts were rewarded with a new contract to stay at the 49ers worth millions of dollars.

But Colin Kaepernick's name isn't associated with Super Bowls or mega-contracts. Instead, he's famous for a simple act of defiance that generated headlines around the world. As the national anthem played at the start of every NFL game in the 2016 season, Colin would sit down or kneel instead of standing to salute the American flag.

Colin's rise to the top of his game came at a time of great social unrest in the USA. Incidents of police brutality against young black men, reported on the nightly TV news, led many black and mixed-race Americans to take to the streets protesting against racial inequality. Amid all this Colin, a mixed-race young man, chose his own demonstration.

'I am not going to stand up to show pride in a flag for a country that oppresses black people and people of colour,' he said. His protest was designed to make racial injustice a hot topic in American society, and with NFL games broadcast into the homes of millions of fans, it certainly sparked a nationwide debate.

Those who supported Colin bought his replica football shirt, making it the country's bestseller. But many disagreed with him and he even received death threats. Nevertheless, Colin kept on kneeling and soon other NFL players joined him. Before long, athletes from different sports were adopting similar protests – and so did many of their fans.

The 49ers didn't renew Colin's contract in 2017, and when he approached other NFL teams, none of them chose to employ him. At the moment, Colin's bravery seems to have cost him a career playing the game he loved. So instead of playing football, he spends his days running community programmes that teach young Americans from disadvantaged backgrounds about their legal rights.

B. 1987

'I have to stand up for people that are oppressed. If they take football away, I know that I stood up for what is right.'

70

MESSI

Footballer and Philanthropist

It's hard to believe that one of the world's greatest footballers, Lionel Messi, almost had to abandon the game before his career even began. To date, Leo has won five Ballon d'Or awards for being the best footballer of the year, a feat matched only by Cristiano Ronaldo. He has won 30 trophies with his club, Barcelona, and has broken countless records – but it could all have been very different.

Leo grew up in Rosario, Argentina, and always loved playing football. From an early age, it was clear that he had the potential to be a skilful player. But when doctors discovered that he had a medical condition that stunted the growth of his bones, his future in football was in doubt. If Leo wanted to continue playing, he would have to inject growth hormones into his legs every single evening. However, the treatment was very costly, and Leo's parents could ill afford it.

Fortunately for Leo, that's when Barcelona FC came calling. Their coach couldn't believe how good Leo was aged only 13. He took Leo and his dad for lunch and agreed to pay for Leo's injections if he would join the team on the spot. Without hesitation, Leo signed the contract the coach had hastily drawn up on a napkin.

It was a humble start for a man who would become one of the world's most admired footballers. But Leo's experiences as a child, when illness and financial difficulties almost shattered his dreams, have made him determined to help others as much as he can. He spends much of his spare time and money supporting disadvantaged children through his Leo Messi Foundation, which aims to help kids achieve their dreams regardless of their circumstances. Leo has visited the sites of earthquakes to help fund rebuilding projects, has travelled to Thailand to play football with young people living with disabilities and has helped to build 20 classrooms for schools in war-torn Syria.

He continues to excite his fans around the world on the pitch, but one thing's for sure: there's a whole lot more to good guy Leo than just being a brilliant footballer.

B. 1987

BOYEGA

Actor and All-Round Good Guy

John is known to many as the character Finn, a Stormtrooper who becomes a rebel pilot in the Star Wars films *The Force Awakens* and *The Last Jedi*. But despite his mega movie star status, John has never forgotten where he comes from.

When John found out that he had won the role of Finn after seven months of auditions, he went straight home to tell his parents. He expressed his gratitude in a traditional Nigerian way, by bowing down to them with his hands on their feet, letting them know how grateful he was for everything they'd done for him. Since then, he's invited his parents to all the premieres for his new movies, and he used the fortune he earned from Star Wars to buy them their first house.

John grew up in Peckham, south London, and he's never wanted to leave – in fact, he still lives just 20 minutes from where he spent his childhood. He's a patron of the Peckham theatre school that offered him a scholarship when he was nine years old, and he regularly promotes local causes. John is also extremely proud of his Nigerian roots, and his production company is committed to developing stories from his parents' homeland. He enjoys introducing traditional Nigerian cuisine to movie-star friends such as Harrison Ford.

John faced racism when some Star Wars fans abused him for playing the first-ever black Stormtrooper. John responded by telling the racists to 'Get used to it'. A passionate believer in equality, he took a similar approach when a group of men protested about the number of women appearing in Star Wars. Pointing out how ridiculous their complaints were, John just laughed at them. He has also spoken up about the lack of diversity in Hollywood and on TV shows, calling upon directors to hire more actors of colour.

Despite his many acts of kindness, John is reluctant to be thought of as a hero by his fans. 'Know the person is a human being and that they can fail at times,' he says, preferring to be known as someone who is never going to be perfect but who tries his best. That's what makes him one of the good guys.

B. 1992

ACKNOWLEDGEMENTS

Thank you to Liza Miller and Debbie Foy at Wren & Rook for making it all happen. Thanks also to Paul Blow for bringing *The Good Guys* to life in such a wonderful way. I'd also like to thank Harry Pearson and the countless authors, biographers and reporters for supplying the research material for these stories of great kindness. Thanks as well to Torre, Caroline, Rory, Bethan and Karen for all their questions – and to Amanda for all of her answers. Thanks to the children of Worple Primary School in Isleworth and to Stanley for the inspiration and motivation.

Rob Kemp

I would like to thank Wren & Rook (Laura) and We Mean This (Matt) for trusting me to deliver 50 portraits – a minor miracle! Also my agent Stu at Handsome Frank, the epitome of handsome, as well as my wife Suzanna and my children Howie and Kitty. And in answer to their daily question, yes, I have finished the 50 portraits – group hug.

Paul Blow

ABOUT THE AUTHOR

....

ROB KEMP

Rob Kemp gave up his job in a magazine office to become a stay-at-home dad soon after his son was born. He has never looked back. Inspired by his son, he has written several books and many articles about fatherhood, raising children and men's health issues. He loves books, finding out about history and doing sports, including cycling, running and football. Rob also helps children at his son's primary school to develop their reading.

....

PAUL BLOW

Paul Blow is an illustrator and wannabe good guy. He draws pictures for magazines all around the world, from *The New York Times* (in New York) to *Greenpeace Magazin* (in Germany). He says coming up with the ideas for the pictures is the hard bit but colouring them in is the fun bit, so colouring in 50 pictures of 50 Good Guys was REALLY fun. Paul lives in Dorset, UK, with his wife Suzanna (also an illustrator) and his two children Howie and Kitty. And their favourite thing to do? Colouring in? No, eating chocolate ice cream.

SOURCES

Confucius

Ames, Roger T. "Confucius." *Encyclopaedia Britannica*, 13 April 2018. https://www.britannica.com/biography/Confucius, accessed 2 May 2018.

"Confucius Biography." *Biography.com*. A&E Television Networks, 15 February 2018. https://www.biography.com/people/confucius-9254926, accessed 2 May 2018.

Leonardo Da Vinci

Isaacson, Walter. *Leonardo da Vinci*. London: Simon & Schuster, 2017.

Leonard, Tom. "Leonardo da Vinci's War Machines Were Failures By Design." *The Telegraph*, 10 December 2002. https://www.telegraph.co.uk/news/uknews/1415660/Leonardo-da-Vincis-war-machines-were-failures-by-design.html, accessed 3 January 2018.

Pierpont, Claudia Roth. "The Secret Lives of Leonardo da Vinci." *New Yorker*, 16 October 2017. https://www.newyorker.com/magazine/2017/10/16/the-secret-lives-of-leonardo-da-vinci, accessed 5 January 2018.

Williamson, Forschungsmitarbeiter Mitch. "Da Vinci's Military Thoughts." *Weapons and Warfare*, 28 October 2015. https://weaponsandwarfare.com/2015/10/28/da-vincis-military-thoughts/, accessed 3 January 2018.

Bartolomé de las Casas

Dussel, Enrique. "Bartolomé de Las Casas." *Encyclopaedia Britannica*, 15 August 2017. https://www.britannica.com/biography/Bartolome-de-Las-Casas, accessed 12 January 2018.

Richard Martin

Isacat, Ben. "Chapter 7: Richard Martin (1754–1834)." *How to Do Animal Rights*, April 2008. http://www.animalethics.org.uk/i-ch6-4-martin.html, accessed 27 January 2018.

William Wilberforce

Abolitionism and Why It Was Opposed | History - Britain's Forgotten Slave Owners. BBC Teach, 18 August 2016. https://www.youtube.com/watch?v=ITtNDpkW26c.

BBC History staff. "William Wilberforce (1759–1833)." BBC History, 2014. http://www.bbc.co.uk/history/historic_figures/wilberforce_william.shtml, accessed 4 March 2018.

Pierard, Richard. "William Wilberforce and the Abolition of the Slave Trade: Did You Know?" *Christianity Today*, 53, 1997. https://www.christianitytoday.com/history/issues/issue-53/william-wilberforce-and-abolition-of-slave-trade-did-you.html, accessed 5 March 2018.

"William Wilberforce (1759–1833): The Politician." *The Abolition Project*. E2BN - East of England Broadband Network and MLA East of England, 2009, http://abolition.e2bn.org/people_24.html, accessed 4 March 2018.

Pierre Toussaint

Pierre Toussaint No. 1–6. New-York Historial Society Museum & Library, 30 May 2008. https://www.youtube.com/watch?v=pHM0DDMfB5Q&list=PL9602F2DF6083BAE4.

"Pierre Toussaint." *Slavery and Remembrance*. The Colonial Williamsburg Foundation, n.d. http://slaveryandremembrance.org/people/person/?id=PP051, accessed 2 February 2018.

Robert Owen

"Robert Owen and New Lanark: A Man Ahead of His Time." *Robert-Owen.com*. New Lanark Trust, n.d. http://www.robert-owen.com/, accessed 12 February 2018.

Robert Owen Museum staff. "Welcome." *Robert Owen Museum*, n.d. http://robert-owen-museum.org.uk/, accessed 12 February 2018.

Simkin, John. "Robert Owen." *Spartacus Educational*. Spartacus Educational Publishers Ltd., n.d. http://spartacus-educational.com/IRowen.htm, accessed 12 February 2018.

Louis Braille

BBC News Magazine staff. "Why Braille is Brilliant." *BBC News Magazine*, 2 January 2009. http://news.bbc.co.uk/1/hi/magazine/7807217.stm, accessed 10 February 2018

Editors of Encyclopaedia Britannica. "Louise Braille." *Encyclopaedia Britannica*, 1 December 2017. https://www.

britannica.com/biography/Louis-Braille, accessed 10 February 2018.

Freedman, Russell. *Out of Darkness: The Story of Louis Braille*. Massachusetts: Houghton Mifflin Harcourt, 1999.

Graves, Dan. "Blind Louis Braille Gave Reading to the Blind." *Christianity.com*. Salem Web Network, 28 April 2010. https://www.christianity.com/church/church-history/timeline/1801-1900/blind-louis-braille-gave-reading-to-the-blind-11630360.html, accessed 11 February 2018.

Abraham Lincoln
"Abraham Lincoln." *Biography.com*. A&E Television Networks, 12 April 2018. https://www.biography.com/people/abraham-lincoln-9382540, accessed 23 April 2018.

BBC History staff. "Abraham Lincoln (1809–1865)." *BBC History*, 2014. http://www.bbc.co.uk/history/historic_figures/lincoln_abraham.shtml, accessed 5 April 2018.

Current, Richard N. "Abraham Lincoln." *Encyclopaedia Britannica*, 12 April 2018. https://www.britannica.com/biography/Abraham-Lincoln, accessed 23 April 2018.

Joseph Rowntree
Joseph Rowntree Foundation staff. "Our Heritage." *Joseph Rowntree Foundation*, n.d. https://www.jrf.org.uk/about-us/our-heritage, accessed 18 February 2018.

The Rowntree Society staff. "Joseph Rowntree (1836–1925)." *The Rowntree Society*, n.d. https://www.rowntreesociety.org.uk/history/rowntree-a-z/joseph-rowntree-1836-1925/, accessed 19 February 2018.

Wainwright, Martin. "Joseph Rowntree's Moral High Road." *The Guardian*, 21 January 2005. https://www.theguardian.com/uk/2005/jan/21/ruralaffairs.martinwainwright, accessed 18 February 2018.

Ferdinand Buisson
Abrams, Irwin. *The Nobel Peace Prize and the Laureates: An Illustrated Biographical History, 1901–2001*. Massachussets: Science History Publications, 2001.

Editors of Encyclopaedia Britannica. "Ferdinand-Édouard Buisson." *Encyclopaedia Britannica*, 14 February 2018. https://www.britannica.com/biography/Ferdinand-Buisson, accessed 3 April 2018.

"Ferdinand Buisson – Facts." *Nobelprize.org*. Nobel Media AB, 2014. https://www.nobelprize.org/nobel_prizes/peace/laureates/1927/buisson-facts.html, accessed 3 April 2018.

Fridtjof Nansen
"Fridtjof Nansen – Biographical." *Nobelprize.org*. Nobel Media AB, 2014. https://www.nobelprize.org/nobel_prizes/peace/laureates/1922/nansen-bio.html, accessed 11 January 2018.

Fridtjof Nansen Biography. UNHCR, the UN Refugee Agency, 10 January 2017. https://www.youtube.com/watch?v=SAUtBFDBCXI

Sverdrup, Harald Ulrik. "Fridtjof Nansen." Encyclopaedia Britannica, 10 October 2017. https://www.britannica.com/biography/Fridtjof-Nansen, accessed 11 January 2018.

Carl Gustaf Emil Mannerheim
Editors of Encyclopaedia Britannica. "Carl Gustaf Mannerheim." *Encyclopaedia Britannica*, 29 May 2015. https://www.britannica.com/biography/Carl-Gustaf-Emil-Mannerheim, accessed 28 January 2018.

Haltzel, Michael. "Unrecognized Courage." *Huffington Post*, 13 April 2017. https://www.huffingtonpost.com/entry/unrecognized-courage_us_58efcfc8e4b048372700d695, accessed 28 January 2018.

Mannerheim authors. "Civilian." *Mannereheim.fi*. n.d. http://www.mannerheim.fi/08_sivil/e_siviil.htm, accessed 29 January 2018.

Mannerheim authors. "Finnish Red Cross: Civilian." *Mannerheim.fi*. n.d. http://www.mannerheim.fi/08_sivil/e_spr.htm, accessed 29 January 2018.

Vihavainen, Timo. "How Mannerheim Helped Finland Earn Its Independence." *thisisFINLAND*. Ministry for Foreign Affairs, June 2017. https://finland.fi/life-society/mannerheim-hero-in-finland-and-russia/, accessed 28 January 2018.

Albert Einstein
"Albert Einstein." *Biography.com*. A&E Television Networks, 20 December 2017. https://www.biography.com/people/albert-einstein-9285408, accessed 29 December 2017.

"Albert Einstein – Biographical." *Nobelprize.org*. Nobel Media AB, 2014. https://www.nobelprize.org/nobel_prizes/

physics/laureates/1921/einstein-bio.html, accessed 29 December 2017.

"Albert Einstein, Civil Rights Activist." *Snopes,* 20 June 2015. https://www.snopes.com/fact-check/einstein-at-lincoln/, accessed 28 December 2017.

Oskin, Becky. "6 Ways Albert Einstein Fought for Civil Rights." *Live Science,* 5 March 2015. https://www. livescience.com/50051-albert-einstein-civil-rights.html, accessed 28 December 2017.

Rovito, Markkus. *Einstein in His Own Words: 100+ Quotes (Albert Einstein Quotes).* California: Hyperink Inc., 2012.

John Flynn
Editors of Encyclopaedia Britannica. "John Flynn." *Encyclopaedia Britannica,* 10 March 2017. https://www. britannica.com/biography/John-Flynn, accessed 5 March 2018.

"History." *Royal Flying Doctor Service.* n.d. https://www. flyingdoctor.org.au/about-the-rfds/history/, accessed 4 March 2018.

"John Flynn (1880–1951)." *ABC.net.* n.d. http://www.abc.net. au/btn/v2/australians/flynn.htm, accessed 4 March 2018.

Ludwig Guttman
BBC Two staff. "Ludwig Guttman and the First Paralympic Games." *BBC Two, 2018.* http://www.bbc.co.uk/ programmes/profiles/3NVTMSLr2ZT9XSFQzYYbcwf/ ludwig-guttman-and-the-first-paralympic-games, accessed 7 April 2018.

"Sir Ludwig Guttman." *Visit Jewish London,* Jewish Committee for the London Games. n.d. http://www. visitjewishlondon.com/jewish-olympics-and-paralympics/ sir-ludwig-guttman, accessed 7 April 2018.

Tanni Grey-Thompson on Sir Ludwig Guttmann, Founder of the Paralympic Games. British Academy, 6 November 2015. https://www.youtube.com/watch?v=s6iAwMdLT4E

Vinegar, Dick. "A Sincere and Heartfelt Homage to the Founder of the Paralympics." *The Guardian,* 10 September 2012. https://www.theguardian.com/healthcare-network/2012/sep/10/homage-founder-paralympics, accessed 7 April 2018.

Learie Constantine
"Lord Leary Constantine." *100 Great Black Britons,* n.d. http://www.100greatblackbritons.com/bios/lord_leary_ constantine.html, accessed 10 February 2018.

Pearson, Harry. Connie: The Marvellous Life of Learie Constantine. London: Little, Brown, 2017. **Charles Drew**
"Charles Drew." *Biography.com.* A&E Television Networks, 19 January 2018. https://www.biography.com/people/ charles-drew-9279094, accessed 8 April 2018.

Dhadon, Dhadon. "Drew, Charles R. (1904–1950)." *BlackPast.org.* n.d. http://www.blackpast.org/aah/drew-charles-r-1904-1950, accessed 8 April 2018.

Oskar Schindler
Anderson, Stuart. "Oskar Schindler: The Untold Story." *Forbes,* 19 March 2014. https://www.forbes.com/sites/ stuartanderson/2014/03/19/oskar-schindler-the-untold-story-3/#41a23cd55537, accessed 7 February 2018.

Schindler's List. Directed by Steven Spielberg. Amblin Entertainment, 1993.

United States Holocaust Memorial Museum. "Oskar Schindler." *Holocaust Encyclopedia,* n.d. https://www. ushmm.org/wlc/en/article.php?ModuleId=10005787, accessed 7 February 2018.

Raoul Wallenberg
Brown, Rob. "The Swedish Schindler Who Disappeared." *BBC News Magazine,* 1 February 2015. http://www.bbc. co.uk/news/magazine-30934452, accessed 30 April 2018.

President Obama Honors Raoul Wallenberg. *WH.Gov,* 2012. https://www.youtube.com/watch?v=gYk4YoGyoVM

Raoul Wallenberg - If You Save One Life, You Save the Whole World. Riddle Films, 8 July 2016. https://www. youtube.com/watch?v=m4KytJNxGAE

United States Holocaust Memorial Museum. "Raoul Wallenberg and the Rescue of Jews in Budapest." *Holocaust Encyclopedia,* n.d. https://www.ushmm.org/wlc/en/article. php?ModuleId=10005211, accessed 7 February 2018.

Jonas Salk
"John Salk." *Biography.com.* A&E Television Networks,

27 April 2017. https://www.biography.com/people/jonas-salk-9470147, accessed 14 February 2018.

Palmer, Brian. "Jonas Salk: Good at Virology, Bad at Economics." *Slate*, 13 April 2014. http://www.slate.com/articles/technology/history_of_innovation/2014/04/the_real_reasons_jonas_salk_didn_t_patent_the_polio_vaccine.html, accessed 14 February 2018.

The Search for the Polio Vaccine. Modern Marvel on History Channel, 5 October 1997.

Quora. "How Much Money Did Jonas Salk Potentially Forfeit By Not Patenting The Polio Vaccine?" *Forbes*, 9 August 2012. https://www.forbes.com/sites/quora/2012/08/09/how-much-money-did-jonas-salk-potentially-forfeit-by-not-patenting-the-polio-vaccine/#369ca36769b8, accessed 14 February 2018.

Nelson Mandela
Editors of Encyclopaedia Britannica. "Nelson Mandela." *Encyclopaedia Britannica,* 28 November 2017. https://www.britannica.com/biography/Nelson-Mandela, accessed 16 February 2018.

Mandela, Nelson. *Long Walk to Freedom*. London: Little, Brown, 1994.

Nelson Mandela's Empathy and Kindness to a Fellow Prisoner at Robben Island Prison. *Pepperdine Law*, 20 September 2016. https://www.youtube.com/watch?v=LoKv8vK5vfU

Nsehe, Mfonobong. "19 Inspirational Quotes from Nelson Mandela." *Forbes*, 6 December 2013. https://www.forbes.com/sites/mfonobongnsehe/2013/12/06/20-inspirational-quotes-from-nelson-mandela/#5b4d77f17101, accessed 18 February 2018.

Smith, David. "Nelson and Winnie Mandela's Marriage Ended, But the Bond Was Never Broken." *The Guardian*, 6 December 2013. https://www.theguardian.com/world/2013/dec/06/nelson-winnie-mandela-marriage, accessed 16 February 2018.

Wooldridge, Mike. "Mandela Death: How He Survived 27 Years in Prison." *BBC News*, 11 December 2013. http://www.bbc.co.uk/news/world-africa-23618727, accessed 16 February 2018.

Edmund Hillary
Editors of Encyclopaedia Britannica. "Sir Edmund Hillary." *Encyclopaedia Britannica*, 12 October 2017. https://www.britannica.com/biography/Edmund-Hillary, accessed 18 February 2018.

Himalayan Trust staff. "About Sir Edmund Hillary." *Himalayan Trust*, n.d. http://himalayantrust.org/about-sir-ed/, accessed 18 February 2018.

Roberts, David. "Everest 1953: First Footsteps - Sir Edmund Hillary and Tenzing Norgay." *National Geographic Adventure*, April 2003. https://www.nationalgeographic.com/adventure/features/everest/sir-edmund-hillary-tenzing-norgay-1953/, accessed 18 February 2018.

David Attenborough
A Message from Sir David Attenborough - Blue Planet II: Episode 7 - BBC One. BBC, 10 December 2017. https://www.youtube.com/watch?v=unOqVELbTr0

Editors of Encyclopaedia of Britannica. "David Attenborough." *Encyclopaedia Britannica*, 11 January 2018. https://www.britannica.com/biography/David-Attenborough, accessed 20 February 2018.

Lawson, Mark. "David Attenborough's Greatest Rescue: Saving Wildlife TV From Extinction." *The Guardian*, 17 November 2016. https://www.theguardian.com/tv-and-radio/2016/nov/17/david-attenborough-planet-earth-ii-secret-life-of-the-zoo-saving-wildlife-tv-from-extinction, accessed 20 February 2018.

Sir David Attenborough on Cambridge's Conservation Hub Building Carrying His Name. University of Cambridge, 6 April 2016. https://www.philanthropy.cam.ac.uk/file/323052, accessed 8 May 2018.

"Sir David Attenborough." *Wood Land Trust*, n.d. https://www.worldlandtrust.org/patrons/sir-david-attenborough/, accessed 20 February 2018.

Martin Luther King Jr
Carson, Clayborne and David L. Lewis. "Martin Luther King, Jr." *Encyclopaedia Britannica*, 15 December 2017. https://www.britannica.com/biography/Martin-Luther-King-Jr, accessed 23 February 2018.

History.com staff. "Civil Rights Act of 1964." *History.com*. A&E Networks, 2010. https://www.history.com/topics/black-history/civil-rights-act, accessed 22 February 2018.

King, Jr., Martin Luther. *The Autobiography of Martin Luther King, Jr.* London: Little, Brown, 2000.

Kirk, Dr John A. "Did Martin Luther King Achieve His Life's Dream?" *BBC*, n.d. http://www.bbc.co.uk/timelines/z86tn39, accessed 22 February 2018.

Meroney, John. "What Really Happened Between J. Edgar Hoover and MLK Jr." *The Atlantic*, 11 November 2011. https://www.theatlantic.com/entertainment/archive/2011/11/what-really-happened-between-j-edgar-hoover-and-mlk-jr/248319/, accessed 22 February 2018.

Barcelona U12 Youth Team
Reuters. Barcelona Under-12s Console Japanese Squad After Beating Them in World Challenge. *The Guardian*, 31 August 2016. https://www.theguardian.com/football/video/2016/aug/31/barcelona-youth-team-console-japanese-squad-soccer-world-challenge-video

Boyan Slat
"About." *The Ocean Cleanup*, n.d. https://www.theoceancleanup.com/about/, accessed 2 April 2018.

Coates, Ashley. "Ocean Plastic Cleanup: A 23-year-old's Mission to Take Rubbish Out of Our Seas." The *Independent*, 7 August 2017. https://www.independent.co.uk/environment/ocean-plastic-cleanup-rubbish-seas-take-out-23-year-old-boyan-slat-north-sea-pacific-microplastics-a7880321.html, accessed 2 April 2018.

Dylan Mahalingam
Yang, Mindy. "Amazing Kids Spotlight Interview with Dylan Mahalingam." *Amazing Kids Magazine*, September 2011. http://mag.amazing-kids.org/non-fiction/interviews/amazing-kids-interview/amazing-kids-spotlight-interview-with-dylan-mahalingam/, accessed 4 April 2018.

Iqbal Masih
Bergmar, Magnus. "Iqbal Masih." *The World's Children's Prize*, n.d. http://worldschildrensprize.org/iqbal-masih, accessed 4 April 2018.

Krtin Nithiyanandam
Davis, Nicola. "Rising Stars of 2017: Research Scientist Krtin Nithiyanandam." *The Guardian*, 1 January 2017. https://www.theguardian.com/science/2017/jan/01/rising-stars-2017-research-scientist-krtin-nithiyanandam, accessed 4 April 2018.

Matthew Kaplan
"About the People." *The Be One Project*, 2018. http://www.thebeoneproject.org/about-the-people/, accessed 5 April 2018.

Toner, Kathleen. "A Brother's Plight Inspires an Anti-Bullying Mission." *CNN*, 14 October 2016. https://edition.cnn.com/2016/10/13/us/cnn-hero-matthew-kaplan-be-one-project/index.html, accessed 5 April 2018.

Moin Younis
Pride of Britain staff. "Teenager of Courage: Moin Younis." *Pride of Britain*, 2017. http://www.prideofbritain.com/history/2017/moin-younis, accessed 6 April 2018.

Rene Silva
Johns, Rafael. "One Teen's News Startup In A Favela." *Huffington Post*, 6 December 2017. https://www.huffingtonpost.com/youth-radio-youth-media-international/one-teens-news-startup-in_b_8842358.html, accessed 6 April 2018.

Richard Turere
Turere, Richard. "My Invention That Made Peace with Lions." *TED Talk*, February 2013. https://www.ted.com/talks/richard_turere_a_peace_treaty_with_the_lions.

Ryan White
"Who Was Ryan White?" *HRSA*, 2016. https://hab.hrsa.gov/about-ryan-white-hivaids-program/who-was-ryan-white

Fred Hollows
Doolan, Brian. "Fred Hollows Foundation Funds Australia's First Indigenous Ophthalmologist." *The Sydney Morning Herald*, 2 October 2014. https://www.smh.com.au/opinion/fred-hollows-foundation-funds-australias-first-indigenous-ophthalmologist-20141002-10p5k0.html, accessed 17 April 2018.

Johnson, Michael. "Obituary: Professor Fred Hollows." *The Independent*, 20 February 1993. https://www.independent.co.uk/news/people/obituary-professor-fred-hollows-corrected-1473050.html, accessed 17 April 2018.

The Fred Hollows Foundation staff. "Where it Began." *The Fred Hollows Foundation*, n.d. https://www.hollows.org/au/what-we-do/indigenous-australia/where-it-began, accessed 17 April 2018.

Harvey Milk
Chandler, Adam. "The Reverse March for Harvey Milk." *Tablet*, 28 November 2012. http://www.tabletmag.com/scroll/117776/the-reverse-march-for-harvey-milk, accessed 19 April 2018.

"Harvey Milk." Biography.com. *A&E Television Networks*, 29 July 2016. https://www.biography.com/people/harvey-milk-9408170, accessed 19 April 2018.

Tavaana staff. "Bringing People Hope: Harvey Milk and the Gay Rights Movement in America." *Tavaana*, n.d. https://tavaana.org/en/content/bringing-people-hope-harvey-milk-and-gay-rights-movement-america-0, accessed 19 April 2018.

The Activism of Harvey Milk. Austin Crittenden on YouTube, 23 June 2010. https://www.youtube.com/watch?v=eXUc2CpioDA

"The Official Harvey Milk Biography." *MilkFoundation.org*. n.d. http://milkfoundation.org/about/harvey-milk-biography/, accessed 19 April 2018.

Selby, Jenn. "People Harvey Milk Day: Why the Former Wall Street Banker is Still the Most Influential LGBT Activist – 37 Years After His Murder." *The Independent*, 22 May 2015. http://www.independent.co.uk/news/people/why-harvey-milk-is-still-the-most-influential-lgbt-activists-36-years-after-his-murder-9413006.html, accessed 19 April 2018.

Mikhail Gorbachev
BBC History staff. "Mikhail Gorbachev." *BBC History*, 2018. http://www.bbc.co.uk/history/people/mikhail_gorbachev, accessed 22 April 2018.

Eaton, William J. "Gorbachev Calls Stalin Crimes 'Unforgivable' : But He Praises Decisions to Collectivize Farms and Push for Rapid, State-Run Industrialization."

Los Angeles Times, 3 November 1987. http://articles.latimes.com/1987-11-03/news/mn-18452_1_soviet-leader, accessed 22 April 2018.

Editors of Encyclopaedia Britannica. "Mikhail Gorbachev." *Encyclopaedia Britannica*, 23 February 2018. https://www.britannica.com/biography/Mikhail-Gorbachev, accessed 22 April 2018.

Taubman, William. *Gorbachev: His Life and Times*. London: Simon & Schuster, 2017.

José Mujica
Davies, Wyre. "Uruguay Bids Farewell to Jose Mujica, its Pauper President." *BBC News*, 1 March 2015. http://www.bbc.co.uk/news/world-latin-america-31679475, accessed 14 April 2018.

The Poorest President. *SBS Dateline*, 23 September 2014. https://www.youtube.com/watch?v=YFSmaztcP4c

Tremlett, Giles. "José Mujica: is This the World's Most Radical President?" *The Guardian*, 18 September 2014. https://www.theguardian.com/world/2014/sep/18/-sp-is-this-worlds-most-radical-president-uruguay-jose-mujica, accessed 14 April 2018.

Murray, Lorraine. "José Mujica." *Encyclopaedia Britannica*, 14 December 2015. https://www.britannica.com/biography/Jose-Mujica, accessed 14 April 2018.

World's 'poorest president' Uruguay's José Mujica & his $1m VW. *BBC News*, 7 November 2014. https://www.youtube.com/watch?v=JqhCAORmsaE

Tenzin Gyatso, 14th Dalai Lama
Best moments from Dalai Lama's press conf. at Council of Europe. Euronews, 15 September 2016. https://www.youtube.com/watch?v=I-KTTtztfhs

"Brief Biography." *His Holiness the 14th Dalai Lama of Tibet*, n.d. https://www.dalailama.com/the-dalai-lama/biography-and-daily-life/brief-biography, accessed 16 January 2018.

"Dalai Lama." *Biography.com*. A&E Television Networks, 27 April 2017. https://www.biography.com/people/dalai-lama-9264833, accessed 16 January 2018.

"Earth Day: Dalai Lama and the Environment." *His Holiness the Dalai Lama's 80th Celebration,* 22 April 2015. http://dalailama80.org/day-5/, accessed 16 January 2018.

James Harrison
Bushak, Lecia. "'Man With The Golden Arm': Rare Blood Type Allows James Harrison To Donate Blood To 2 Million Babies." *Medical Daily*, 16 June 2015. https://www.medicaldaily.com/man-golden-arm-rare-blood-type-allows-james-harrison-donate-blood-2-million-babies-338416, accessed 23 January 2018.

MacDonald, Fiona. "Australian Man's Blood Donations Have Saved 2 Million Lives." *Science Alert*, 11 June 2015. https://www.sciencealert.com/australian-man-s-blood-donations-have-saved-2-million-lives, accessed 23 January 2018.

"Pioneer of Australia's Anti-D Plasma Program." *Australian Red Cross Blood Service*, n.d. https://www.donateblood.com.au/learn/anti-d/james-harrison, accessed 23 January 2018.

Patrick Stewart
ComicPalooza Sir Patrick Stewart Part 1. Oswald Vinueza, 26 May 2013. https://www.youtube.com/watch?v=ZPWkLOestks

Low, Valentine. "Horrors of War Drove My Father to Violence, Says Patrick Stewart." *The Times*, 12 May 2014. https://www.thetimes.co.uk/article/horrors-of-war-drove-my-father-to-violence-says-patrick-stewart-kg8mfz58rnp, accessed 2 February 2018.

"Patrick Stewart." *Biography.com*. A&E Television Networks, 4 February 2016. https://www.biography.com/people/patrick-stewart-522668, accessed 2 February 2018.

Sir Patrick Stewart Reveals the Domestic Violence He Witnessed as a Child | Loose Women. Loose Women, 12 April 2018. https://www.youtube.com/watch?v=QQ9oIl1q69c

Muhammad Ali
Bulman, May. "Muhammad Ali Dead: The Boxing Icon Explains His 'Recipe for Life.'" *The Independent*, 4 June 2016. http://www.independent.co.uk/news/people/muhammad-ali-dead-interview-recipe-for-life-dies-aged-74-a7065416.html, accessed 4 February 2018.

Callahan, Maureen. "How Muhammad Ali Secured the Release of 15 US Hostages in Iraq." *New York Post*, 29 November 2015. https://nypost.com/2015/11/29/the-tale-of-muhammad-alis-goodwill-trip-to-iraq-that-freed-us-hostages/, accessed 4 February 2018.

Hauser, Thomas. *Muhammad Ali: A Tribute to the Greatest*. London: HarperSport, 2016.

"Muhammad Ali." *Biography.com*. A&E Television Networks, 18 January 2018. https://www.biography.com/people/muhammad-ali-9181165, accessed 4 February 2018.

Tallent, Aaron. "Muhammad Ali's Kindness was Legendary." *Athlon Sports*, 6 June 2016. https://athlonsports.com/life/muhammad-alis-kindness-was-legendary, accessed 4 February 2018.

Ban Ki-Moon
Alexander, Harriet. "What Has Ban Ki-moon Done for the World?" *The Telegraph*, 20 September 2016. https://www.telegraph.co.uk/news/0/what-has-ban-ki-moon-done-for-the-world/, accessed 11 February 2018.

"Ban Ki-moon." *United Nations*, n.d. https://www.un.org/sg/en/formersg/ban.shtml, accessed 11 February 2018.

Steinecke, Kai. "UN Chief Ban Ki-moon Leaves Behind a Mixed Legacy." *DW*, 13 December 2016. http://www.dw.com/en/un-chief-ban-ki-moon-leaves-behind-a-mixed-legacy/a-36752578, accessed 11 February 2018.

Christopher Reeve
"Christopher Reeve." *Biography.com*. A&E Television Networks, 29 December 2014. https://www.biography.com/people/christopher-reeve-9454130, accessed 12 February 2018.

Christopher Reeve Last Public Speech at Rehabilitation Institute of Chicago 10-04-2004. *Aura De Leon*, 25 October 2008. https://www.youtube.com/watch?v=4z507jWH2Kc&t=264s

"Our Story." *Christopher & Dana Reeve Foundation*, n.d. https://www.christopherreeve.org/about-us/our-story, accessed 12 February 2018.

Tim Berners-Lee
"Biography." *W3.org*. n.d. https://www.w3.org/People/Berners-Lee/, accessed 15 February 2018.

"Sir Tim Berners-Lee." Web Foundation, n.d. https://webfoundation.org/about/sir-tim-berners-lee/, accessed 15 February 2018.

Bill Gates

"Bill Gates." *Biography.com*. A&E Television Networks, 30 April 2018. https://www.biography.com/people/bill-gates-9307520, accessed 2 May 2018.

"Bill Gates Profile." *Forbes*, n.d. https://www.forbes.com/profile/bill-gates/, accessed 2 May 2018.

Martin, Emmie. "The Simple Reason Why Bill Gates is No Longer the Richest Person in the World." *CNBC*, 10 January 2018. https://www.cnbc.com/2018/01/10/why-bill-gates-is-not-the-richest-person-in-the-world.html, accessed 2 May 2018.

Ai Weiwei

"Ai Weiwei: China's Dissident Artist." *BBC News Asia*, n.d. http://www.bbc.co.uk/news/world-asia-pacific-12997324, accessed 28 April 2018.

Tate Modern staff. "Interpretation Text." *Tate*, n.d. http://www.tate.org.uk/whats-on/tate-modern/exhibition/unilever-series/unilever-series-ai-weiwei-sunflower-seeds/unilever, accessed 28 April 2018.

Weiwei, Ai. "Ai Weiwei: The Artwork That Made Me the Most Dangerous Person in China." *The Guardian*, 15 February 2018. https://www.theguardian.com/artanddesign/2018/feb/15/ai-weiwei-remembering-sichuan-earthquake, accessed 28 April 2018.

Barack Obama

"Barack Obama." *Biography.com*, 9 March 2018. https://www.biography.com/people/barack-obama-12782369, accessed 4 April 2018.

Maraniss, David. *Barack Obama: The Story*. London: Simon & Schuster, 2013.

President Obama's Best Moments with Little Kids. Celebrity101, 10 December 2016. https://www.youtube.com/watch?v=cbKwfY3ThhE

Younge, Gary. "Yes, He Tried: What Will Barack Obama's Legacy Be?" *The Guardian*, 19 May 2016. https://www.theguardian.com/us-news/2016/mar/19/yes-tried-barack-obama-legacy-gary-younge, accessed 4 April 2018.

George Michael

BBC News staff. "George Michael's Philanthropy Comes to Light After His Death." *BBC News*, 27 December 2016. http://www.bbc.co.uk/news/uk-38442559, accessed 5 December 2017.

Sweeting, Adam. "George Michael Obituary." *The Guardian*, 26 December 2016. https://www.theguardian.com/music/2016/dec/26/george-michael-obituary-wham-pop-star, accessed 5 December 2017.

Elon Musk

Bereznak, Alyssa and Kate Knibbs. *"The Great Elon Musk Debate."* The Ringer, 13 September 2017. https://www.theringer.com/tech/2017/9/13/16302426/elon-musk-villain-hero, accessed 17 December 2017.

"Elon Musk." *Biography.com*. A&E Television Networks, 15 March 2017. https://www.biography.com/people/elon-musk-20837159, accessed 18 December 2017.

Light, Larry. "Tesla, SpaceX, A.I., Mars and More: Is Elon Musk Spread Too Thin?" *CBS News*, 16 May 2017. https://www.cbsnews.com/news/elon-musk-spread-thin-tesla-space-x-mars-artifical-intelligence/, accessed 17 December 2017.

Smith, Andrew. "Who is Elon Musk? Tech Billionaire, SpaceX Cowboy, Tesla Pioneer – and Real Life Iron Man." *The Telegraph*, 24 May 2017. https://www.telegraph.co.uk/technology/0/elon-musk-tech-billionaire-spacex-cowboy-real-life-iron-man/, accessed 17 December 2017.

Vance, Ashlee. *Elon Musk: How the Billionaire CEO of SpaceX and Tesla is Shaping Our Future*. London: Virgin Books, 2015.

Jamie Oliver

Barr, Sabrina. "Don't Assume Obese Poor People Lack Willpower, Says Jamie Oliver." *The Independent*, 5 March 2018. http://www.independent.co.uk/life-style/health-and-families/jamie-oliver-obesity-poor-disadvantaged-people-willpower-healthy-diet-report-a8240076.html, accessed 10 April 2018.

Jamie's Food Revolution staff. "About." *Jamie's Food Revolution* n.d. http://www.jamiesfoodrevolution.org/about, accessed 10 April 2018.

SOURCES

Jamie's Ministry of Food Rolls into Australia's 3rd Largest Aboriginal Community. Jamie's Ministry of Food Australia, 9 September 2015. https://www.youtube.com/watch?v=PXfla-2irvA

Jamie Oliver Visits Ministry of Food Australia. Jamie Oliver, 26 April 2012. https://www.youtube.com/watch?v=aYZ0gcWpOO4

Benedict Cumberbatch
Goodfellow, Jessica. "UN Women UK Turn Words into Actions With #drawaline Campaign to End Violence Against Women." *The Drum,* 25 November 2017. http://www.thedrum.com/news/2017/11/25/un-women-uk-turn-words-actions-with-drawaline-campaign-end-violence-against-women, accessed 26 March 2018.

Lewis, Justin. *Benedict Cumberbatch: The Biography.* London: John Blake Publishing Ltd, 2014.

Murray, Lorraine. "Benedict Cumberbatch." *Encyclopaedia Britannica,* 15 November 2017. https://www.britannica.com/biography/Benedict-Cumberbatch, accessed 26 March 2018.

The Best You staff. "It's Elementary: a Benedict Cumberbatch Interview." *The Best You Magazine,* 24 October 2014. https://thebestyoumagazine.co/its-elementary-a-benedict-cumberbatch-interview/, accessed 26 March 2018.

Yorke, Tom. "Benedict Cumberbatch." *Interview Magazine,* November 2017. https://www.interviewmagazine.com/film/benedict-cumberbatch-november-2017-issue, accessed 26 March 2018.

John Green
"About John Green." *John Green Books,* n.d. http://www.johngreenbooks.com/bio, accessed 7 March 2018.

Earl, Evangeline. "My Sister Esther Inspired 'The Fault in Our Stars.' The Movie is Her Sequel." *The Washington Post,* 12 June 2014. https://www.washingtonpost.com/opinions/my-sister-esther-inspired-the-fault-in-our-stars-the-movie-is-her-sequel/2014/06/12/504c2ca4-efef-11e3-914c-1fbd0614e2d4_story.html?utm_term=.61e1ac62a735, accessed 7 March 2018.

Project for Awesome staff. "About." *Project for Awesome,* n.d. http://www.projectforawesome.com/about, accessed 7 March 2018.

Didier Drogba
BBC News staff. "Didier Drogba Seeks to Bring Peace to Ivory Coast." *BBC News,* 21 September 2011. http://www.bbc.co.uk/news/world-africa-15001107, accessed 6 May 2018.

Didier Drogba Talks About His Charity. Sam Mole (SportsMole.co.uk), 18 January 2013. https://www.youtube.com/watch?v=yAnnKAopcHM

How the World Cup Stopped a War. COPA90, 15 July 2017. https://www.youtube.com/watch?v=n7GUCESwD3g

Special Olympics staff. "Football (Soccer) Legend Didier Drogba Announced as Special Olympics' Newest Global Ambassador." *PR Newswire,* 2 May 2018. https://www.prnewswire.com/news-releases/football-soccer-legend-didier-drogba-announced-as-special-olympics-newest-global-ambassador-300641139.html, accessed 6 May 2018.

Professor Green
Manderson, Stephen. "Men Shouldn't Suffer in Silence with Depression and Anxiety." *The Guardian,* 20 August 2014. https://www.theguardian.com/commentisfree/2014/aug/20/men-suffer-depression-anxiety, accessed 22 February 2018.

Weale, Sally. "Professor Green: White Working-class Boys Becoming More Disengaged." *The Guardian,* 7 January 2018. https://www.theguardian.com/society/2018/jan/07/professor-green-white-working-class-boys-becoming-more-disengaged, accessed 22 February 2018.

Usain Bolt
First Post staff. "Usain Bolt Insists to Shoot all Advertisements in Jamaica to Give Back to His Community." *First Post,* 21 July 2016. https://www.firstpost.com/sports/usain-bolt-insists-to-shoot-all-advertisements-in-jamaica-to-give-back-to-his-community-2906428.html, accessed 1 March 2018.

Thomas, Claire. "10 Facts You Didn't Know About Usain Bolt, World's Fastest Man." *The Telegraph.* 3 August 2017. https://

SOURCES

www.telegraph.co.uk/athletics/2017/08/03/10-facts-didnt-know-usain-bolt-worlds-fastest-man/, accessed 1 March 2018.

Wright, Duncan. "Police Block Usain Bolt: Police Made Me Stop Giving My Money Away Because It Was Causing Too Many Fights in Jamaica." *The Sun*, 30 June 2016. https://www.thesun.co.uk/sport/1362742/usain-bolt-police-made-me-stop-giving-my-money-away-because-it-was-causing-too-many-fights-in-jamaica/, accessed 1 March 2018.

Colin Kaepernick
Branch, John. "The Awakening of Colin Kaepernick." *New York Times*, 7 September 2017. https://www.nytimes.com/2017/09/07/sports/colin-kaepernick-nfl-protests.html, accessed 30 April 2018.

Editors of GQ. "Colin Kaepernick Will Not Be Silenced." *GQ*, 13 November 2017. https://www.gq.com/story/colin-kaepernick-will-not-be-silenced, accessed 30 April 2018.

Colin Kaepernick Explains Why He Won't Stand During National Anthem. *KTVU*, 29 August 2016. https://www.youtube.com/watch?v=ka0446tibig

Norman, Fox. "NFL Players Slam Owners in Heated Meeting for Leaving Colin Kaepernick 'Hung Out to Dry,' Report Says." *Fox News*, 25 April 2018. http://www.foxnews.com/sports/2018/04/25/nfl-players-slam-owners-in-heated-meeting-for-leaving-colin-kaepernick-hung-out-to-dry-report-says.html, accessed 30 April 2018.

Lionel Messi
Gibbs, Dan. "Lionel Messi: Barcelona Star Makes Incredible Gesture to Charity." *The Express*, 3 November 2017. https://www.express.co.uk/sport/football/875264/Lionel-Messi-Barcelona-charity-Doctors-Without-Borders, accessed 4 March 2018.

Lowe, Sid. "Lionel Messi: How Argentinian Teenager Signed for Barcelona on a Serviette." *The Guardian*, 15 October 2014. https://www.theguardian.com/football/blog/2014/oct/15/lionel-messi-barcelona-decade, accessed 3 March 2018.

Messi Meets His Biggest Fan - the Plastic Bag Boy (The Story of Murtaza Ahmadi). 21stCenturyFootball, 13 December 2016. https://www.youtube.com/watch?v=h9Cc3m6P6jQ

Messi staff. "Bio." *Messi.com*. Leo Messi Management S.L.U. n.d. https://messi.com/bio, accessed 4 March 2018.

Wee, Timothy. "12 Messi Charity Moments." *Fox Sports Asia*, n.d. http://www.foxsportsasia.com/football/742722/12-messi-charity-moments/, accessed 3 March 2018.

John Boyega
Addley, Esther. "John Boyega: from Peckham, to the Death Star, to the Old Vic." *The Guardian*, 21 April 2017. https://www.theguardian.com/film/2017/apr/21/john-boyega-from-peckham-to-the-death-star-to-the-old-vic, accessed 20 April 2018.

Dockterman, Eliana. "A Star of His Own Making." *Time*, 12 October 2017. http://time.com/collection-post/4972291/john-boyega-next-generation-leaders/, accessed 20 April 2018.

Hattenstone, Simon. "John Boyega: I'm Very Direct. I Can't Lie." *The Guardian*, 10 March 2018. https://www.theguardian.com/film/2018/mar/10/john-boyega-star-wars-attack-the-block-film-simon-hattenstone, accessed 20 April 2018.

John Boyega Interview on Star Wars, the Episode 8 Script and Taking Harrison Ford for Dinn. Lloyd Yates (Global Press Conferences), 1 September 2016. https://www.youtube.com/watch?v=d6pbhU6F4FU

John Boyega visits Nigeria. *CNBC Africa*, 3 April 2018. https://www.cnbcafrica.com/videos/2018/04/03/john-boyega-visits-nigeria/

Okonofua, Odion E. "Actor Speaks About His Dropping Out of School to Pursue Acting Career." *Pulse.ng*. 14 April 2018. http://www.pulse.ng/entertainment/celebrities/john-boyega-speaks-about-dropping-out-of-school-for-acting-id8258565.html, accessed 20 April 2018.

INDEX

INDEX